Lean Scaleup

Frank Mattes

Frank Mattes

Lean Scaleup

Co-written with

Hans Balmaekers	innov8rs
Dr. Stefan Biel	Beiersdorf
Steve Cook	bp Launchpad
Daniele Dondi	ING
David Gilmour	bp Launchpad co-founder
Kirsten Grønborg	oktopus
Peter Guse	Vector Informatik (f. Robert Bosch)
Ofer HaCohen	AT&T
Dominick Kennerson	Bayer G4A
Jörg Killer	Lean Scaleup
Sören Jens Lauinger	B. Braun
Christian Lindener	Airbus
André Marquis	UC Berkeley
Brian Mooney	Mach49 / Effectus Research
Rob Munro	Innovation Success
Prof. Dr. Georg Oenbrink	CREAGO Solutions (f. Evonik Industries)
Jon Rains	Mott MacDonald
Jeremy Schönwälder	Henkel
Carina Snijder	Philips
Martin Sondenheimer	Munich Re
Nina Teng	London Business School
Carsten Vogt	Merck

First Edition, May 2021 Independently published

ISBN: 978-3-9823154-2-3

Lean Scaleup

A proven approach
to build new businesses
from innovation

Frank Mattes

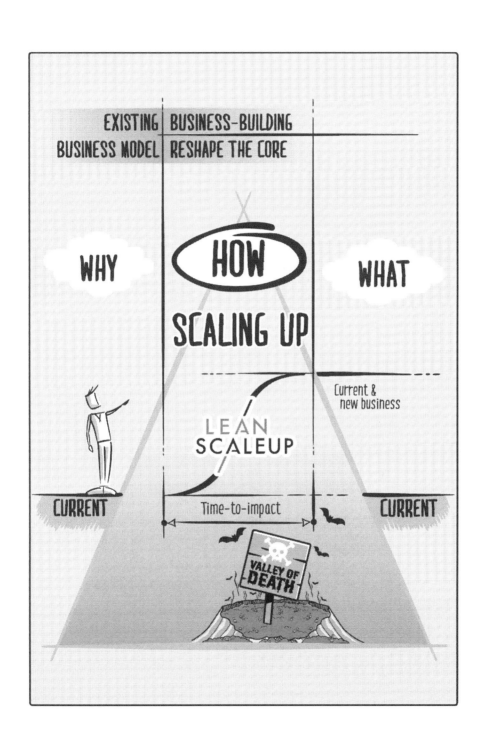

For Tina.
For the ONE.

CONTENTS

113 CHAPTER 07: METHODOLOGY OUTLINE

147 CHAPTER 08: THE PRE-SCALING TEAM AND MINDSET

161 CHAPTER 09: FREQUENT MISTAKES AND BEST PRACTICES

Advance praise for this book

Corporate leaders struggle to find the right balance between "perform" and "transform," between "scale/ efficiency" and "speed/ agility," between running a highly efficient core business while innovating new digital propositions.

Compelling ideas can be developed into new minimally viable propositions, but translating "viable" into "scalable" is challenging, as systems and cultures clash between the core and the new.

Frank Mattes brings his extensive experience in corporate innovation to this pragmatic guide to dramatically increasing return on investment in digital innovation.

Jeroen Tas
Chief Innovation & Strategy Officer, Royal Philips

Frank Mattes has decades of valuable experience in innovation and business-building. This has helped him draw together the key themes, challenges, and solutions for companies needing to transform their businesses through creating value through innovation. He has distilled the key practices that companies need to embrace.

In this time, with the challenges of disruption, the rapid evolution of business models, and the need to re-define the ways business works, the Lean Scaleup provides a route map.

Senior leaders searching for new approaches to drive value in their business, to be better placed to deliver success for themselves, their company, employees, and shareholders can benefit.

The Lean Scaleup is an approach built through practice in the field and results from real work supporting companies facing existential challenges that the market has brought forward.

David Gilmour,
co-founder bp Launchpad

The full value of innovation is reached when it achieves scale. Getting there is one of the greatest challenges of the innovation process. This book provides a practical framework and methodology for going beyond the MVP into scale.

Frank brings his insightful expertise and leverages the experience of corporate innovation leaders, creating a must-read for corporate innovators and leaders.

Ofer HaCohen,
Head of Innovation Center Israel, AT&T

This book is a valuable orientation for every corporate innovator. In this book, experience meets empiricism, helping corporates of all kinds to increase confidence.

Jeremy Schönwälder
Global Open Innovation Lead, Henkel

From the many conversations within our global community of innovation leaders, it has become clear this is one of the most important yet most challenging problems: closing the gap between a validated idea and a solid business line with a substantial impact on the top and bottom line.

Frank has been able to address this issue in many organizations successfully. I'm excited for his approach to be "codified" in this book finally. I can't recommend Frank and this book enough to every innovation team keen to deliver results.

Hans Balmaekers,
CEO, innov8rs

Lean Scaleup solves an essential part of the corporate innovation problem; how to increase the chances of an innovation win at scale substantially. Corporate Innovators can stop laboring under a false pretense to know their sweat is worth it.

Rob Munro
Founder and Principal Consultant, Innovation Success

As an innovation practitioner, I've read many books about early-stage innovation, but this is the first one about how to scale MVPs – highly recommended for practitioners – and their managers!

Kirsten Grønborg
CEO, oktopus

The why, what and how of corporate innovation at scale - Frank expertly bridges the chasm with practical examples in business language. Highly recommended.

Jon Rains
Director, Mott MacDonald Ventures

Corporates usually fail to scale and grow new business ventures outside their existing portfolio of products, services, and solutions successfully. The Lean Scaleup approach from Frank Mattes gives them a viable and powerful tool to identify, develop and scale breakthrough innovations very successfully and sustainably for the first time. This book is a must-read for all managers from corporate innovation or strategic innovation.

Prof. Dr. Georg Oenbrink,
CEO, CREAGO Solutions (formerly Evonik industries)

The most challenging phase in new business creation is the Scaling-Up phase. This book provides an excellent framework to address this challenge and is based on the real-life learning journey of +20 corporates, including Philips. A must-read for corporate entrepreneurs and their leaders!

Carina Snijder, VP,
Head of Research Program Management
and Business Development, Royal Philips

Frank is a great expert in the field of corporate venture building. His experience in scaling is a huge source of practical inspiration. This book provides a great framework for corporates who are seriously looking to convert innovation investments into business impact.

Daniele Dondi
Lead CoE Business Design & Ops at ING Neo

Lean Scaleup is a practical how-to guide to make an impact happen. Frank Mattes has combined his extensive corporate innovation experience with the solid groundwork of analyzing leading companies to find the ingredients that make the magic of scalability real. It is THE super-relevant challenge in today's businesses.

Sören Lauinger
VP Cooperations, Innovations & Interfaces, B. Braun Group

Before you start

Dear Valued Reader,

Thank you very much for your interest in this book.

My sincere wish is that you find value in it and that it helps you sharpen your thinking on how to build new businesses from innovation.

To get the most out of this book, you might find it valuable to take a look at a sequence of short videos that I have prepared. These give you a condensed overview of this book's main thoughts. You will find them at:

https://www.leanscaleup.com/book-1-videos

Furthermore, to help you advance your discussions, I have prepared a Microsoft PowerPoint presentation, including some worksheets. This presentation will give you an indication if your company has a business-building problem. You will find it at:

https://www.leanscaleup.com/book-1-worksheet

On each of these pages, you will also find the opportunity to message me directly. I am looking forward to hearing your thoughts and to many engaging discussions.

Sincerely,

Frank Mattes
Wiesbaden / Germany
May 2021

Chapter

01
INTRODUCTION

CHAPTER 01

Introduction

"You read a book from beginning to end.
You run a business the opposite way.
You start with the end, and then
you do everything you must to reach it."

Harold Geneen

One of the world's largest companies asked me to help them understand their specific problems in creating new businesses from innovation.

This company was one of more than 20 that I had gathered to work on what seemed to be a widespread problem: well-running intrapreneurship programs, great innovation ideas, and promising corporate ventures never made it to scale. Most of these ambitions died after the "Minimum Viable Product" stage. They never became a sizable and profitable business.

I was in a conference room, preparing a presentation to the Steering Committee of this project. I wanted my audience to see the essential points that I had discovered in the last two months. **Building a new business from innovation is a complex multi-disciplinary and multi-level play,** and so I spoke with a few dozen corporate stakeholders, corporate startups, corporate ventures, and managers from the functional units that were supposed to collaborate with the corporate startups and ventures.

I flipped through my papers to recall quotes and figures that supported my points. A Senior Vice President from Corporate R&D said, "it takes us ages to make some baby steps. We need to transform the enterprise – but we will never make it if we continue with this pace." He showed me a list of initiatives. "This one could generate more than USD 100m annually in value. That one could revolutionize a whole industry. We cannot let them sit around."

I remembered his concerns when we started to work. "If we do not improve our business-building capability, our company will only have the M&A option for its corporate transformation – but this is a costly and risky route."

I saw the notes of a meeting with the leader of a corporate startup. He said, "I need to spend a quarter of my time fighting for funding and working corporate politics. We are not moving at startup speed. We have to discuss every decision with our governance board. We meet them once per month for two hours. But most of the time, we are discussing 'the plan.' We are fighting hard in the market – and we are fighting internally as well. We fight a two-front war."

I went through a list that I had compiled to understand the magnitude of my client's business-building problem. It showed their non-incremental innovation initiatives from five years ago and the investments into these activities. Five years is a typical time-to-impact timeframe – so these initiatives should now generate revenues. But for every 100 dollars that the company spent back then, they make 7 dollars now. The company was not making money from innovation; it was burning money. Some companies are doing far worse – a logistical company gets only 1.50 dollars per 100 dollars invested. But this was certainly not a reason for my client to feel satisfied.

As the room filled up, I had a final glance at the notes from the meeting with the CEO of a corporate venture. He said, "corporate is treating us like we are an established, large-sized company. They do not get the difference between the running business and innovation. Working with corporate functions is a nightmare. They do not understand what we are doing. We are always at the bottom of their priority lists, and they find tons of reasons why they can't work with us in a startup way."

What is this book about?

This book aims at solving one of the biggest problems in corporate innovation. **Companies are doing okay in small-step, incremental innovation, by which they generate additional business in their existing business**

areas – studies[1] show a failure rate of 40-60 percent. **But they struggle dramatically in non-incremental innovation** – several studies (see chapter 2) see a failure rate of 85-90 percent. In other words, corporates grow their business – and their staff – by exploiting a successful value proposition. **They are good at copying past success stories but bad at creating new ones.**

If companies do not solve this problem, they will:

– burn money

– fail to achieve revenue growth from innovation

– fail in corporate transformation

– fail to future-proof their business

– fail in winning and retaining top talent

This book shows that companies who have been through disruption, or fear being disrupted, have **a powerful way to create new businesses**. It guides corporate innovators and leaders of corporate startups/ventures (short: "EBOs" which stands for "emerging business opportunities") through the non-linear, muddy, and sometimes confusing torrent called innovation.

These men and women are heroes. They want to create a piece of the company's future – a new business which in some cases is even new to the industry or the world. They jump into wild waters and navigate uncertain territory where there is no corporate procedure telling them what to do to succeed. They deserve to have the best tools and the proper support from the company. When they do, they can safely reach the other side of the wild river – and the company, in return, gets a new business with new revenues and a piece of the transformation agenda.

To the best of my knowledge, the book shows the first framework for building a new business in a corporate context with a complete end-to-end journey, from a "meaningful idea" to a sizable business. This framework is called **Lean Scaleup™**. It shows you what steps to take, how to take them, what the company's leadership needs to do, and how to build a supportive, collaborative culture. The framework builds on Best Practices – hence it also

---

1 https://image-src.bcg.com/Images/Managing_the_Unmanageable_Sep_2013_tcm9-93937.pdf

contributes to demystifying innovation success and turning business-building from art to practice.

As shown in chapter 5, the Lean Scaleup™ framework consists of three parts: methodology, or the "how-to" (described in more depth in chapters 7-11); leadership's role; and culture/collaboration. The framework is much more than a box of tools. It **guides companies through the uncertainties of business-building.**

When the right innovation teams use the proper thinking tools with the right mindset (see chapters 7-11) in a supportive environment, the company can solve its business-building problem. Such a supportive environment enables entrepreneurial spirit, deals with the inevitable prioritization issues effectively, and connects corporate stakeholders and innovators in a meaningful way.

If I look at the enormous global challenges, I see that a lot of innovation is needed. In my view, this "innovation at scale" can only come from large companies. And this is my mission: to help companies find the best innovators, select the right innovations and turn them into significant, sustainable new businesses which reduce – or even overcome – global challenges.

Who should read this book?

This book is highly relevant to four target groups.

Corporate Innovation / Digital Innovation

In many companies, Corporate Innovation and Digital Innovation units drive non-incremental innovation. They do the early-stage work to create strategic options, e.g., conducting R&D and scouting for, investing in, and onboarding external startups. They select the EBOs that should be accelerated and taken to scale, and provide support to their founders and leaders.

These two types of units live in a paradoxical situation. They have to secure resources for EBOs with a potentially high value but with a high uncertainty profile. These EBOs compete for funding and resources against corporate initiatives in the core business that have a lower value but a "calculable" risk. But due to the inherent uncertainty of innovation, the corporate innovators can provide solid value proof points only after the new business has been created. Up until that point, there are many assumptions. And **since the new business is unfamiliar to the corporate stakeholders, there are as many opinions about these assumptions' validity as there are people in the room.**

This book is designed to answer the many questions of corporate innovators and managers of Digital Innovation units:

- Which of the many options on the table should we double down on?

- Should we invest in a specific concept and take it to scale?

- How do we achieve alignment between Core and the new business that we are building?

- How can we ensure a meaningful pathway for an EBO after the technical pilot?

- How can we build a new business out of our cutting-edge technology?

- What are effective thinking tools, and what is the right team and mindset to apply them?

- What helpful language and narrative should we use to help leadership understand the business-building problem and what they need to do to solve it?

Leaders of corporate startups/ventures

Leaders of EBOs are not just entrepreneurs working in large companies. To innovate, they must successfully navigate a complex bureaucracy designed to run an existing business. So their first job is – within this complexity – to create a **"market product"** that is the basis for a new business.

But they also have to build two more products at the same time. In contrast to greenfield startups, corporate startups have only one funding option: the company. Hence, leaders of corporate startups also have to make an investment case – they have to build an **"investor product."** Furthermore, the business they are creating is a part of the corporate transformation, so they also need to create a **"Reshape the Core product."**

This book is also for leaders of EBOs who ponder questions such as:

- What do we need to do on our innovation journey to reduce risk and accelerate the journey?

- How can we best use corporate assets to give us an "unfair advantage" in the market?

- What do we need to do after validating that we are "worthy to be scaled" and "ready to be scaled" to set us up for Scaling-Up success?

- How do we manage hypergrowth in the Scaling-Up phase?

Senior Management

Without the support of leadership, changing how the company builds new businesses will not work. The company extracts money from current operations to fund new businesses. It provides corporate assets (e.g., technical facilities, access to a customer base, and the corporate brand) to make the EBO successful.

If Senior Management has the will to **own the business, both today and in the future**, then it needs to reconcile two conflicting targets: safely delivering short-term cash flows, and creating tomorrow's business. Hence, Senior Management needs to define effective "rules for engagement."

This book is for Senior Managers who work on questions like:

- What do I need to change so that the company improves in building new businesses?

- How should I engage in a meaningful way so that we can run and optimize today's business and create tomorrow's business at the same time?

- What are the arguments I should use in front of line managers about the necessary changes to improve business-building?

Chief Strategy Officers

The strategy function has been the target of much criticism in recent years. The central allegation is that the conventional annual planning process is no longer fit for purpose in today's fast-moving, complex markets. Competition and disruption do not follow a yearly calendar. The separation of strategy formulation from implementation creates delay, undermines organizational ownership, and reduces responsiveness to opportunities.

The challenge for Chief Strategy Officers is designing an alternative strategy process and capability that is better suited to today's disruptive market reality, while simultaneously delivering a plan and framework for capital allocation and value creation in the broader stakeholder sense.

The Lean Scaleup™ offers Chief Strategy Officers a powerful new tool for upgrading strategy work when they work on questions such as:

- How can I build a more dynamic strategy process?

- How can corporate strategy combine strategic learning and realization at the same time?

- How can we substantiate assumptions about future scenarios outside of Core?

Why should you read this book?

In my research, I found well-written cases and studies that investigated the particular issues of building a new business from innovation. There are also excellent books[2] with original thinking that have proven their value. But the points they made are just parts of the puzzle. They do not cover the end-to-end journey from idea to scale, and they do not integrate leadership and culture/collaboration issues.

---

2 Geoffrey Moore, "Crossing the Chasm"; Henry Chesbrough, "Open Innovation"; W. Chan Kim/Renée Mauborgne, "Blue Ocean Strategy"; Steve Blank "Four Steps to the Epiphany"; Eric Ries, "The Lean Startup"; Ash Maurya, "Running Lean"; Bill Aulet; "Disciplined Entrepreneurship"; Alexander Osterwalder, "Business Model Generation," "Testing Business Ideas," and "The Invincible Company"

Many innovation books are ideas books. They provide ideas on how the company could become more innovative. This book is not an ideas book – it is a practical getting-it-done book. It is for practitioners, from practitioners.

To write a book that has the ambition to cover the end-to-end innovation journey would surely be too much for a single person. And actually, this book draws from the experiences and insights of many minds:

–   My clients, corporate and Digital innovators and EBO leaders from a wide range of industries – from Aerospace to Financial Services, from Energy to Chemicals, from MedTech to Automotive

–   Corporate innovators and Digital innovators from more than 20 leading companies who co-created the Lean Scaleup™ framework

–   This book's Advisory Board of forward-thinking practitioners and two leading business schools

Why am I a trusted source of advice?

I think it is remarkable that a Fortune 10 company, a global leader in Aerospace, and a leading Swiss Financial Services company all selected a small consulting agency from Germany to help them think through non-incremental innovation challenges and how to set up for success.

I started in the early 1990s when the term innovation was not yet mainstream (although already discussed by figures such as Peter Drucker and W. Edwards Deming). Back then, most companies used the term "new product development" and waterfall-type project management to "bring the new into the world." At the end of the 1990s, I was working with one of the globally leading consulting firms. We introduced Phase/Gate processes, portfolio management and ran projects that today would be called business model innovation.

Some ten years ago, I founded innovation-3, a consulting agency specializing in non-incremental innovation. Initially, we did a lot of work in open innovation. We searched for external ideas, concepts, and solutions to technical challenges and set up win/win collaborations to make it happen. Around

2015, the "open" was rapidly becoming "Digital," and we ran projects that today are called "service-centered business models."

Around 2017, I noticed that across industries, more and more companies were saying, "we are not short of ideas – but we are not creating business impact." It became clear to me that this problem must be solved, and that it can be solved. Since then, my company and I have focused on helping companies solving their business-building problems.

Since then, in our client assignments, we have worked with several dozens of EBOs and their corporates both directly and indirectly, via the Lean Scaleup™'s co-creation process. I shared the insights that we collected along the way in conferences, podcasts, blog posts, and a preceding book[3].

Lean Startup and Lean Scaleup

At this point, you probably wonder how the Lean Scaleup relates to the Lean Startup. The term "lean" originally comes from the manufacturing industry. Lean is about creating value and eliminating waste to reduce costs and improve efficiency, productivity, and quality. Lean looks at activities and removes as much waste as possible so that the customer gets the most value. However, removing waste does not necessarily mean throwing things away. It instead means taking resources that are not adding value and using them somewhere else, where they add value.

Ten years ago, Eric Ries[4] applied lean principles to the early stages of greenfield startups' innovation journey. The Lean Startup's focus was to avoid building "products that nobody wants" – and subsequently, building a business on those products that customers want.

In the following years, an increasing number of companies saw the Lean Startup as the right tool for the early stage of building new businesses from innovation. The focus was on creating ideas for new businesses and so almost

---

3 Frank Mattes, "Scaling-up Corporate Startups" – see https://www.innovation-3.com/scaling-up-book
4 Eric Ries, "The Lean Starup" and "The Startup Way"

every large company was building innovation centers, digital labs, etc., then. 82 percent of large companies claim to use the Lean Startup today[5].

Despite its widespread adoption. the Lean Startup did not solve the corporate business-building problem. 85-90 percent of EBOs do not make it beyond the "Minimum Viable Product" stage (see chapter 2). So having the right mindset in the early stage of business-building is good – but not good enough.

Consequently, VC firms and companies' focus has shifted towards the later stage of innovation. **Companies have become aware that if they are not good at scaling up great ideas, all early-stage activity is just a costly hobby.** VCs have become aware of the business-building problem, too – two-thirds of the USD 135bn that US VCs invested in 2018 went into scaling successful startups[6].

Consequently, creating business impact from the many early-stage ideas is now predominant on many corporate innovation agendas. Leading companies have found that additional thinking is needed if an EBO is to go beyond the Minimum Viable Product stage (see chapters 2 and 5). The viewing angle needs to be extended. It needs to cover the entire journey, from idea to scale, and to integrate the corporate context, which is a significant opportunity and a substantial challenge for EBOs.

That is why I co-created the Lean Scaleup™ framework, together with more than 20 leading companies from various industries, to ensure that it is a practical and actionable framework with cross-industry relevance. It breaks new ground – but it builds on the Lean Startup, incorporates its foundational principles, and uses terms (such as "Minimum Viable Product") familiar to many corporate practitioners.

---

5 https://www.innovationleader.com/downloadable-documents/lean-startup-in-large-organizations/882.article
6 https://www.mckinsey.com/business-functions/mckinsey-digital/our-insights/the-big-boost-how-incumbents-successfully-scale-their-new-businesses

How can you apply what's inside?

Of course, you should use your professional judgment in applying the content. For instance, the term "Minimum" (as in, Minimum Viable Product) has to be seen in the industry context – one cannot fly with a "minimum viable airplane" because of the regulatory environment of this industry. But an airplane manufacturer might well test prototype interior concepts or pre-production Digital services in a well-defined context.

Companies can benefit from the Best Practices encapsulated in the Lean Scaleup™ framework in three levels, as described in more detail in chapter 6. In increasing order of magnitude – both concerning the efforts necessary and the potential improvements for business-building, these are:

- Applying bits and pieces. This could be, for example, a particular validation method or the checklist to transfer from validation to Scaling-Up, to augment the system already in place

- Applying the Lean Scaleup to one EBO

- Building the "innovation infrastructure beyond the lab"

How is this book organized?

I am a practical guy, and this is a practical book. It will show you a framework to solve the corporate business-building problem with the proper combination of facts, helpful tools, the right mindset, and guidance on the dos and don'ts.

This book has two sections. The first is about the problem to be solved, where this problem comes from, and introduces the Lean Scaleup™ as a solution framework. Section 2 is about the Lean Scaleup methodology – the thinking tools and the "how-to."

Part 1: The problem and the framework

This section starts with nailing down the Scaling-Up problem and why it has to be solved (chapter 2). Chapters 3 and 4 provide effective language to make arguments more precise and more powerful and explain why existing approaches are insufficient. Chapter 5 presents the Lean Scaleup™ framework, and chapter 6 shows three options for how companies can apply it to improve business-building.

Part 2: Lean Scaleup™ methodology

The second section starts with a high-level outline of the Lean Scaleup™ methodology in chapter 7. Chapter 8 is about the right team and mindset to use these thinking tools effectively. Chapter 9 features the ten most frequent mistakes and Best Practices in pre-Scaling that I have seen in my advisory practice.

Chapters 10 and 11 are about the Scaling-up phase. They look into the market- and product-related aspects of scaling and the culture- and people-related aspects. The book concludes with chapter 12, in which I put excellence in Scaling-Up into the context of emerging organizational models.

Some naming conventions

For easier readability, I have made some provisions. Firstly, Lean Scaleup™ is a registered trademark in the European Union and the United States of America. To increase the reading flow, I will skip the trademark sign further down in the text.

"Core" describes the functional units that run the day-to-day business, e.g., Marketing, Sales, Supply Chain/Logistics, Procurement, IT, Finance/Controlling, and HR. Although innovation is organizationally a part of the organization (and there is also innovative work in the functional units above), it helps in thinking through – as explained in chapters 2 and 3 – to separate Core and innovation, even though they are under one roof.

"**Product**" stands for the content of an innovation, which could be a physical product, a service bundle, a bundle of products and services, or a new business model.

Similarly, "**market**" is used to describe the group of "customers" who will want, use, adopt, or somehow engage with the innovation – not necessarily, but in most cases, people with wallets.

And finally, corporate startups/ventures that drive innovation are abbreviated to **EBOs** (short for "emerging business opportunities").

Intellectual Property

All trademark regulations apply to the use of the registered trademark Lean Scaleup.

Concerning Intellectual Property, the Lean Scaleup methodology consists of two parts: tools from third parties that allow public use under a Creative Commons license – such as the Business Model Canvas (CC) Strategyzer.com – and proprietary tools as the 4x4 pre-Scaling matrix shown in chapter 7.

The latter part of tools is made publicly available under a Creative Commons license, (CC) leanscaleup.com. These tools are also open to variations. Where variations are created, the original source must be included in the variation – this means the text leanscaleup.com should be visible and legible under every tool, in its original or an altered form.

The Lean Scaleup visuals in this book and on www.leanscaleup.com are copyrighted. Corporate practitioners and not-for-profit organizations may use them for their internal purposes with due reference to leanscaleup. com. Software companies, service providers (e.g., consulting agencies), and freelancers must obtain explicit permission from the Lean Scaleup company to use them.

Upcoming books

Providing a detailed description for creating new business from innovation with all aspects would be too much for one book. This book is the first one in a series of publications. Three more books are planned:

- Lean Scaleup – Methodology: The Field Book

- Lean Scaleup – Dual Leadership

- Lean Scaleup – Culture and Collaboration

Chapter

02
THE PROBLEM

Six essential insights in this chapter.

You will find these again within the text.

 Corporate innovation needs to insure the company against irrelevance by finding answers to five challenges: (1) blurring industry boundaries; (2) emerging future value pools; (3) the existing business model losing its relevance; (4) service-centered business models gaining in importance; (5) sustainability becoming as essential as financial viability.

 To build new businesses, the company could, in theory, leverage corporate assets for an "unfair advantage" and to accelerate the journey. There are six categories of innovation-relevant intangible assets: operational and functional capabilities; advanced expertise and know-how; growth-enabling capabilities; privileged assets; technology and IT; transactional data.

 Companies do okay when they repeat past success stories, but they cannot create new ones. Within the proven, existing business model, they achieve a 40-60 percent success rate. When they try to build new businesses outside their core, this success rate drops to 10-15 percent.

 The business-building problem is a Scaling-Up problem.

The Scaling-Up problem has three root causes: (1) two incompatible management systems are supposed to work together; (2) during Scaling-Up, the EBO travels from one system to another through a White Space; (3) one crucial dimension is missing in the approaches companies use to structure the pre-Scaling phase.

 There are seven more causes for the Scaling-Up problem that can be traced back directly or indirectly to the root causes: (1) incompatible governance and KPIs; (2) different clock speeds; (3) Scaling-Up requires special people; (4) no solid model that can be taught; (5) organizational inertia; (6) limited access to corporate assets and the two-front war; (7) no shared view on the Scaling-up problem.

 Solving the "Scaling-Up problem" is the prerequisite for solving the business-building problem.

There are three reasons why a company must solve its Scaling-up problems: (1) achieving "Return On Innovation"; (2) succeeding in corporate transformation; (3) winning in the war for talent.

CHAPTER 02

The Problem

*"If you don't like to embrace business-building,
you are going to like irrelevance even less."*

Frank Mattes

Innovation certainly does not suffer from management attention. It has a high priority in almost any company – BCG and McKinsey found independently that 7 out of 10 CEOs consider innovation a top-3 priority.

One reason is that excellence in innovation correlates with business success. Many studies have shown that innovation leaders have higher revenue growth and margins than their peers. They also have a higher market capitalization. According to Forbes' annual list of the most innovative companies, innovation leaders have a 70-90 percent "innovation premium." This premium is the bonus that investors pay because they expect these companies to continue their innovation leadership.

Innovation, the insurance against irrelevance

There is a second reason why innovation is high on corporate priority lists. Excellence in innovation provides insurance against irrelevance and protection against commoditization. Statistical data[7] shows that the average lifespan of companies is decreasing:

---

7 https://www.aei.org/

— 89 percent of the companies on the 1955 Fortune 500 list are not on the current list.

— Companies in the 1965 S&P 500 stayed in the index for an average of 33 years. By 1990, this average was 20 years, and it is forecasted to shrink to 14 years by 2026.

— At the current churn rate, half of today's S&P 500 firms will be replaced in the next ten years.

— It is reasonable to assume that in the 2080 Fortune 500 list, almost all of today's companies will no longer exist.

Companies need to reevaluate – and potentially redefine – their business against five forces shaping their business context. These could lead to irrelevance. In my advisory work, I discuss five forces frequently:

— Industry boundaries blur

— Future value pools emerge

— The existing business model loses its relevance

— Service-centered business models gain in importance

— Sustainability becomes as essential as financial viability

Industry boundaries blur

A brilliant example of the speed and impact of industry convergence is the Southeast Asian Internet economy. Not everyone might be familiar with this business arena. A Google study[8] shows that in only four years, the industry landscape has completely changed. In 2015, companies from different industries were focused solely on their respective industries. Fast forward to 2019 – now, players from all sectors compete fiercely against each other in all industries.

Blurring industry boundaries do not reshape industries; they unshape them. Established players lose their positions, and new winners emerge who

---

8 https://www.blog.google/documents/47/SEA_Internet_Economy_Report_2019.pdf; the visual mentioned is on page 43

serve the customer base with new value propositions created and delivered in new value chains.

The blurring of industry boundaries does not necessarily require Digital. For example, a client of mine ponders how to react to Food and Healthcare's converging to Functional Foods. But **in most situations, Digital is the primary driver**, such as Advanced Mobility, Smart Grids, Telemedicine – or Amazon moving into everything, from retail to movies to cloud services and logistics.

In this theme, corporate innovators need to insure the company against irrelevance in at least four ways by:

- Anticipating where industry boundaries blur and new value pools emerge
- Identifying emerging value chains and define pivotal positions
- Capturing the value via new offerings and business models
- Making new capabilities available

Future value pools emerge

Game-changing innovations open future value pools. These innovations fulfill a job-to-be-done much better as before, solve a problem that was never solved before or serve an entirely unaddressed customer base. Five examples may illustrate this point.

Improve the job-to-be-done: Procter & Gamble Swiffer. Swiffer is a line of cleaning products from Procter & Gamble. Its initial product was an electrostatic dust remover, which dramatically improved the job-to-be-done "cleaning floors in the home."

Introduced in 1997, the brand uses the "razor-and-blades" business model. Consumers purchase the handle at a low price, but must continue to buy replacement refills over the product's lifespan. To this day, Swiffer is one of Procter & Gamble's most successful product launches, generating more than USD 500m in sales annually.

Solve an unsolved problem: Nestlé Nespresso. Before Nestlé introduced its capsule-based espresso system, consumers had to make a choice. Either they could get top-tasting, expensive coffee outside of their homes – or they could choose less tasty coffee at home.

Nestlé created a new category by combining convenience-at-home with top taste. It invented a new technical system and a new business model. The technical system consists of two parts: firstly, a coffee machine that generates immense pressure to draw out more flavor from coffee capsules; secondly, the only capsules that fit this machine come from Nestlé[9]. Nespresso bypasses traditional retail and instead relies on its outlets and online commerce/direct-to-consumer shipments. Today, Nespresso sells more than 14 billion capsules annually, and Nespresso brings in more than USD 10bn in revenues.

Solve an unsolved problem: Apple iPod and iTunes. When Steve Jobs introduced iTunes in 2001, he pointed out that current solutions to the job-to-be-done of "managing music for on-the-go" were too complicated and too technical for the average consumer.

Within two years, Apple launched the iPod (the hardware companion) and the iTunes Music Store. This combination offered consumers a convenient way to legally buy digital music assets and the music publishers the reassurance of a Digital Rights Management. With software, hardware, and an online store, Apple established itself as a new intermediary in the music value chain. Ten years after opening the iTunes store, Apple had sold more than 35 billion songs, with 30 percent of the revenue – on average USD 0.99 per piece – flowing into Apple's pockets.

Serve an unaddressed customer base: Amazon Web Services. Amazon Web Services (AWS) is a subsidiary of Amazon. It provides an on-demand cloud computing platform to individuals, companies, and governments on a metered pay-as-you-go basis.

Amazon initially designed AWS as a standardized and automated platform for Amazon's retail computing infrastructure. It then saw the opportunity to generate a new business and have the outside world finance AWS by

---

9 This was the original concept. Since a few years, other companies can also sell caspules that fit the Nespresso coffee machines

opening defined platform layers. In 2004, Amazon launched the first public AWS service. In 2015, AWS became profitable with annual sales of USD 7.8bn. Another four years later, AWS had become a USD 35bn business, generating roughly 71 percent of Amazon's overall operating profits.

Serve an unaddressed customer base: Netflix. In its 25-year history, Netflix – an American media services provider and production company – has transformed its business model several times. When founded in 1997, Netflix was a movie rental service relying on postal mail. Customers ordered DVD movies online and received them via postal mail. After watching the movie. they sent the DVDs back to Netflix.

In 1999, Netflix launched a subscription-based business model. Ten years after its foundation, Netflix innovated its business model again by introducing video streaming. Another four years later, Netflix produced its first original content series. With this step, Netflix moved from being a distribution channel for the major movie studios to a competitor. Today, Netflix has more than 200 million paid subscriptions worldwide.

Improve the job-to-be-done: Hilti Fleet Management. Hilti is a Liechtenstein-based machine supplier to the construction industry who successfully introduced a "power-tool-as-a-service" business model.

The basic fleet management idea at Hilti comes as a one-stop package. Customers can turn tool costs from capital expenditures into operating expenses and save administrative work. A fixed monthly fee covers all expenses related to financing, service/maintenance, and repair.

Some ten years after its introduction, Hilti had more than 1.2m tools under fleet management, representing a contract value of more than USD 1.4bn. As Hilti's CTO stated, "Hilti developed many very innovative and successful products over the years. But they pale in comparison with the fleet management business model, which was the most important innovation in Hilti's history."

In this theme, corporate innovators need to insure the company against irrelevance in three regards by:
 – Identifying emerging value pools

- – Capturing the value in these pools via new offerings and business models

- – Making new capabilities available

The existing business model is losing its relevance

Only one of the innovations mentioned above plays out in the company's existing business model, Procter & Gamble's Swiffer. All other ones were new-to-the-company, new-to-the industry, or even new-to-the-world business models.

The ongoing search for new business models should be on the management agenda. **Companies that regularly rejuvenate their business model portfolio generate more shareholder returns** than those who fixate on the business model that made the company great in the past[10]. Six of the world's ten largest companies are serial business builders, having launched at least five new, significant businesses during the past 20 years.

However, not all companies understand the importance of the continuous search for new business models. One reason might be top management's relentless focus on the day-to-day business – it almost seems that staff is not allowed to think outside the box. Another reason might be that there is something seductive about success. It lures people into thinking that the future will be equal to the past.

Especially for companies that have sustained success over many years, it is hard to imagine that the success might end. But it does stop at times, as we all know:

- – Fortune Magazine wrote in March 1998 a story about "How Yahoo Won the Search Wars," just six months before Google's foundation.

- – In 2017, the Guardian asked, "Will MySpace ever lose its monopoly?" In April 2018, Facebook took the lead in user numbers, and MySpace spiraled into oblivion.

---

10 McKinsey Quarterly, July 2020: Why you've got to put your portfolio on the move

– In November 2007, half a year after Apple introduced the iPhone, Forbes asked, "Nokia. One billion customers – Can anyone catch the cell phone king?" Six years later, Nokia sold off the remains of its col-lapsed cell phone handhelds business.

Disruption rarely comes from the known competitors, as these examples (and many more, e.g., Kodak, Blockbuster, Encyclopedia Britannica, Skype, and LED lighting) show. In some cases, disruption does not even come from a company, but from fundamental changes in customer preferences. For example, Nike tries hard to find answers to video gaming, and meat producers struggle to adjust to rapidly changing consumer preferences.

Even the most profitable business models have life cycles, like products. When they are just budding businesses, developed by a few whiz kids in a garage or a corporate innovation lab, their initial value is tiny. As the business model gains traction, the value grows steeply. Once the underlying technology ages or customer preferences shift over time, the value goes down. Hence the life cycle of a business model follows an s-curve.

Companies need to find a new, sustainable business model in due time. If they fail to do so, they become yet another more data point in the S&P 500 statistics (see above).

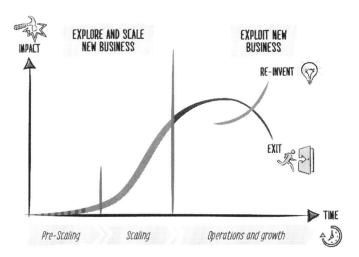

Figure 2-1: Life cycle of a business model

Once "the platform is burning," it may be too late for the aircraft carrier to change its course and build the capabilities for success in a changing environment. Hence, starting the search for a new profitable business model needs to begin well before the existing one declines. It should be an ongoing process, which further helps prepare for unexpected strikes from unknown vectors.

In this theme, corporate innovators need to insure the company against irrelevance in at least two regards by:

– Identifying new business models that could become a sizable and sustainable business for the company

– Leveraging corporate assets (see below) for an "unfair advantage" in building these new businesses and accelerate their journey

Service-centered business models gain in importance

A particular business model type has gained significant traction in the last years. In so-called service-centered business models, companies switch from selling products to providing customers with a convenient service that offers a practical, one-stop-shop solution to their jobs-to-be-done.

Service-centered business models have revenue models that significantly differ from product-based business models. Typically, services are charged via monthly subscriptions or metered usage. Hilti's Fleet Management (see above) or aircraft engine maker Rolls-Royce's "TotalCare" plan – in which airline customers pay per flying hour – are examples of service-centered business models and their revenue models.

Service-centered business models have a financial and a strategic rationale. The financial motivation is to provide a steady income stream for ongoing contracts, improve resilience during global crises, and increase product life cycles. The strategic rationale is to increase customer lock-in. When customers are satisfied with the service, they have only a few incentives to switch, and switching costs are high. In other words, service-centered business models increase the customer's barrier to exit and the company's competitive advantage.

Service-centered business models offer the company insurance against irrelevance. But they are hard to implement. Corporate innovators need to work hard to implement them:

- They build heavily on Digital for (a) connecting products and sub-services that make up the offer, (b) providing the base for predictive maintenance, and (c) using customer data to generate insights that help to anticipate customer needs and to provide a superior experience.

- They require deep domain expertise to understand the customer's job-to-be-done and the customer journey profoundly – only then can an excellent solution be designed and implemented.

- They demand require extreme validation rigor and complete alignment of corporate functions and ecosystem capabilities.

Sustainability becomes as essential as financial viability

From a linear, profit-maximizing management thinking, when the daily pressures of generating cash flow guide every boardroom decision, it might be understandable that business leaders see environmental sustainability as a secondary priority.

However, the role of business in society has evolved. Investors, customers, employees, public authorities, and the public demand more. Business is more than just generating profits and jobs; it is also about environmental sustainability and ethical business practices. In other words, stakeholders expect companies to have a meaningful purpose that transcends business operations and purely financial results.

For example, several investors today use Environmental, Social, and Governance (ESG) metrics – such as a company's carbon footprint, water usage, community development efforts, and board diversity – to evaluate a company. Research shows[11] that companies with high ESG ratings have a lower cost of debt and equity, and that sustainability initiatives can help improve financial performance while fostering public support.

---

11 Devalle, A. et al.: The Linkage between ESG Performance and Credit Ratings. International Journal of Business and Management. 12. 53. 10.5539/ijbm.v12n9p53.

Consequently, a growing number of firms integrate sustainability into their business strategy. They see that they can solve some growth problems while at the same time making a positive impact on the planet and can better meet their stakeholders' expectations when sustainability and good ethics are closer to the Core.

In this theme, corporate innovators need to insure the company against irrelevance by launching new offerings and business models that are financially viable and – at the same time – environmentally sustainable.

Here comes the business-building problem

These five themes put two fundamental questions to companies and corporate innovators on the table:

- — What new businesses should the company create?
- — What should the company do to create these businesses with a good level of certainty?

At a high flight altitude, there are three potential solutions. Firstly, corporate innovation could work with external startups or integrate the technology and talent from a startup acquisition. This strategy is not easy. Only 1 out of 12 companies consider their relationships with startups to be very satisfying[12]. Weaving acquired external startups into the corporate fabric is also not an easy task. Statistically, 50 percent of an acquired startup's top talent has left the company after two years[13].

The second option is that the company could acquire innovative, established businesses. After the acquisition, corporate innovation would use the acquired business' technology and talent to deliver the innovation agenda. This approach is a risky business. M&A failure rates are between 70-90

---

12 https://www.bcg.com/de-de/publications/2019/corporate-startup-relationships-work-after-honey-moon-ends

13 https://mitsloan.mit.edu/ideas-made-to-matter/your-acquired-hires-are-leaving-heres-why

percent[14], and studies show[15] that organic growth generates more value than acquisitions.

Thirdly, the company could build business-building capabilities. Success in this option builds on corporate innovation's ability to implement a robust validation and scaling framework and create a supportive environment for EBOs – for which the Lean Scaleup provides the playbook. Statistically, this is the best of organic growth options[16] – and organic growth creates more value than M&A (see above).

However, companies struggle dramatically in creating new businesses from innovation.

Theoretically, there is an unfair advantage

Established companies in many industries are fighting against VC-backed greenfield startups. While the chances for an individual "greenfield startup" to build a sizable business are low, the VCs that back them have large portfolios and deep pockets. So how should companies with a limited portfolio and a limited budget win this competition?

The answer is to move fast and smart, by leveraging corporate assets. Large, established companies have a broad base of assets that a VC-backed "greenfield startup" can only dream of. Some of these assets are tangible (physical) assets, such as production facilities and owned points-of-sales. Others are intangible assets (i.e., assets that do not show up on the balance sheet) which could be highly relevant for innovation.

Aside from **funds and talent**, intangible assets can, in many cases, be the source of an "unfair advantage" in building a sizable business and accelerating the journey. Access to an existing customer base, for example, can lower the customer acquisition costs and accelerate market uptake. I see six categories of **innovation-relevant intangible assets**:

---

14 https://hbr.org/2011/03/the-big-idea-the-new-ma-playbook
15 https://www.mckinsey.com/business-functions/strategy-and-corporate-finance/our-insights/the-value-premium-of-organic-growth
16 ibidem

Operational and functional capabilities such as Sales, Supply Chain Management, Procurement, Production and Quality Management, Financial Controlling, IT, Legal, Intellectual Property, Recruiting, HR, and Regulatory Affairs provide functional expertise.

Advanced expertise and know-how such as market insights, models for risk and fraud detection, Artificial Intelligence and Machine Learning models, and cybersecurity enable cutting-edge Digital solutions.

Growth-enabling capabilities such as large-scale contracts to source licenses, resources, raw materials, components, interim human resources, online and offline marketing expertise, growth hacking capabilities, access to influencers, opinion leaders, and regulators accelerate the Scaling-Up journey.

Privileged assets such as brand and reputation, access to customers, channel partners and ecosystems, initial customer base (in business-to-consumer plays: employees as customers), and Intellectual Property (including patents and trade secrets) provide differentiation options and accelerate the journey.

Technology and IT comprising individual technologies, technology platforms, and technology toolkits (such as Volkswagen's MQB toolkit for e-vehicles), IT for transactional purposes (such as existing SAP systems), safety and security systems, and Machine Learning / Artificial Intelligence platforms reduce investments and unit costs during Scaling-Up.

Transactional data enables fast and effective statistical analysis and training of Artificial Intelligence models.

Some of these intangible assets should be in every innovation, as when none of these assets are used in an innovation, the company effectively builds a venture in the wild. In this case, corporate innovators will not have a convincing answer to the question, "why should our company do this innovation and not someone else?"

For an individual innovation, these corporate assets might be real game-changers, leveraged without significant considerations ("no brainers"), or might be used with careful consideration ("trade-offs").

But companies do not materialize the unfair advantage

There is probably no business area that has absorbed more attention, books, blogs, and conferences over the last few years than innovation. But there is perhaps no business area where the gap between ambition and results is more massive.

 Companies are doing okay with small-step, incremental innovation. Within the proven, existing business model, they manage to get a 40-60 percent success rate (see above). But they struggle dramatically when they aim to build new businesses outside of their core from their non-incremental innovation activities. They are not able to turn their potential unfair advantage into a winning proposition. In other words, companies are doing okay when they repeat past successes, but they cannot create new ones.

Here are some statistics that highlight the disappointing situation:

- Only 1 of 8 corporate startups achieve scale[17].

- Only 1 of 20 business innovations are successful[18].

- 84 percent of executives say that innovation is critical for their business, but only 6 percent are satisfied with the outcome[19].

- Only 10 percent of companies with Digital Innovation units have successfully scaled their ideas up into a launched product[20].

- 54 percent of executives believe that getting ideas to market quickly and at scale is the number one innovation problem[21].

- Only 20 percent of Chief Strategy Officers see their company prepared for disruption[22] .

17 https://hbr.org/2016/12/when-large-companies-are-better-at-entrepreneurship-than-startups

18 https://www.bcg.com/de-de/publications/collections/most-innovative-companies-2018

19 https://www.mckinsey.com/business-functions/strategy-and-corporate-finance/how-we-help-clients/growth-and-innovation

20 https://www.strategyand.pwc.com/gx/en/insights/2019/strategists-guide-to-digital-innovation.html

21 https://www.capgemini.com/de-de/wp-content/uploads/sites/5/2020/09/Final-Web-Report-Scaling-innovation.pdf

22 https://www2.deloitte.com/us/en/insights/topics/leadership/chief-strategy-officer-survey.html

These statistics spell disaster for many companies. When they cannot build new business, they will fall prey to the five forces shown at the beginning of this chapter. They will become another company that "did not make it."

The business-building problem is not a problem that only large corporates face – it also applies to medium-sized companies. Conventional wisdom suggests that smaller companies are better in innovation because they are faster and more agile in their decision-making, and their organization is less bureaucratic. They are supposed to be closer to the customer, and are less tied to existing technology and infrastructure. Furthermore, since they are more often privately owned, they have a longer time horizon and do not have to eye the quarterly analyst calls. However, a study found[23] that company size is not a differentiator. In other words, **smaller companies are not significantly better at building new businesses than large corporates.**

Does your company have a business-building problem?

At https://www.leanscaleup.com/book-1-worksheet you will find a presentation and worksheets, that will indicate if your company has a business-building problem.

There is a multi-million-dollar question on the table for most companies, in the most genuine sense of the words: Why can't companies turn more of their innovation concepts into sizable and profitable businesses?

My clients are either aware of their business-building problem or want to accelerate in business-building success. When I begin work, I strive to align with the stakeholders on the magnitude of their company's business-building problem. I often use **four probing questions to start the conversation.**

---

23 https://www.bcg.com/en-ca/publications/2020/most-innovative-companies/overview

What is the financial impact of past activities?

A quick litmus test provides insight into the financial magnitude of a company's business-building problem. It looks at a 3-5-year horizon since this is a typical time for non-incremental innovation to generate revenues:

- Which innovation initiatives aimed at creating new products, services, and business models did the company pursue 3 to 5 years ago?

- How much money (cash out) did the company spend on these activities?

- How much revenue do these initiatives generate today?

This analysis generally leads to some surprises. For every dollar spent five years ago, one of my clients created revenues of 7 cents and another client of 1.5 cents. In these companies, innovation did not generate money; it burnt significant money. Of course, such results are not acceptable. After becoming aware of these figures, both companies started to solve their respective business-building problems immediately.

How high is Core's management attention for innovation?

Another valuable metric for starting the conversation is the percentage of senior managers' time spent creating new business. Typically, this percentage is tiny, and activities center around participating in governance boards.

The deeper reason is that **senior managers focus – and are rewarded – on the KPIs of the existing day-to-day business.** So, although innovation is at the top of the corporate agenda (see above), in practice, senior management's attention is absorbed by keeping the "delivery engine" humming. There is only so much management attention left for the "discovery and business-building engine."

Core's senior managers run their businesses on a 0-3-year timescale. Their focus is on real operating priorities, performance management, and risk management. The bulk of just the operational challenges and the ups and downs of a regular business leaves little room for multi-year ambitions such as business-building.

So, creating a new business inevitably slips to the tail end of senior management's agenda. Consequently, this trickles down to the managers who report to them. Their yardsticks for success also measure the short-term performance of the existing business.

EBOs[24] require a lot of care and attention from senior management, and most of my clients are aware of this. But in real life, with harsh prioritization realities, doing two fundamentally different things simultaneously – running and optimizing the existing business and nurturing a future business that might bring in significant contributions in 3-5 years – is almost too much.

How deep is the Valley of Death?

A third valuable metric to start discussing the business-building problem is how many EBOs have died in the recent past. Many EBOs that did not make it to scale (see above) flame out after a particular stage of the innovation journey – the Minimum Viable Product (MVP) stage. **Almost every company has an innovation "Valley of Death" after MVP.** The only difference is how deep this valley is.

Figure 2-2: "Valley of Death"

---

24 "Emerging Business Opportunity" which stands for corporate startup/venture

The fundamental issues mentioned below explain why MVP is the breaking point. MVP marks the beginning of a transitional phase in the innovation journey, in which Core and EBO need to work together. Very few companies have an innovation infrastructure that catapults EBOs through this phase.

Interestingly, the "Valley of Death" also applies to the scaling of Digital technologies inside the company. The World Economic Forum looked into smart factories and their related Internet-Of-Things technology. It found[25] that the most significant barriers to scaling after the MVP stage are the lack of resources and missing knowledge about how to scale.

Does innovation have the proper distance from Core?

A fourth conversation starter about the business-building problem is to discuss the proper distance between Core and innovation. "Distance" in this context refers to physical locations, language, and management processes. This distance is mandatory for separating Core's operating model from innovation's operating model (see chapter 3). Twenty years ago, Tuschman and O'Reilly[26] found that companies who separate operations and innovation get better innovation results. They coined the term "ambidexterity" for such an approach – doing two different things at the same time, "Running/optimizing Core" and "Creating the New."

Many companies followed this approach and set up physically separated innovation centers and Digital labs. If one enters one of these facilities, one can immediately spot the difference. Typically, there is vintage furniture, tons of post-it notes tacked to the walls, an Italian espresso machine, table football, and bean bags – a far cry from the efficiency-oriented and often dull atmosphere in corporate offices.

The language in these innovation units is different. The innovators use terms such as MVP, "disruption", "experiments", "problem/solution-fit", "product/market-fit," "traction", etc. These words are not in the vocabulary of

---

25 https://3q0ds8402hawyzjwb3qrnh43-wpengine.netdna-ssl.com/wp-content/uploads/2018/11/180 1WEFIndstr4.0.pdf

26 O'Reilly III, C. A./ Tushman, M. L. (2008): Ambidexterity as a dynamic capability: Resolving the innovator's dilemma. Research in Organizational Behavior 28 (2008) 185–206.

Core people. So, when innovators approach the core organization, there is a huge language barrier. Often, translation is not working at all, and **both sides find themselves "lost in translation."**

When the distance is too great, it cuts off innovation from corporate decision-making. When innovators work in secluded spaces, using a different language than Core's, they are far from corporate decisions on goals, costs, budgets, productivity, and corporate initiatives.

Embedding innovation into Core is not a panacea, either. Some companies have tried to solve distance-related issues by placing innovation units in the operative units. But there, the innovation teams are exposed continuously to operative decision-makers (see above) and their operative agenda. Often, one finds that the concepts that come out from these embedded innovation units are just so big that the operative units can digest them – but far too small to cope with the five forces shown at the beginning of this chapter.

The business-building problem is a Scaling-Up problem

Scaling-Up is an indispensable part of the innovation journey, which runs from idea to business impact. When the innovation should become a sizable and sustainable new business, it needs to scale. Customers have to buy, value creation and delivery must be managed, and an organization that handles business operations has to be created.

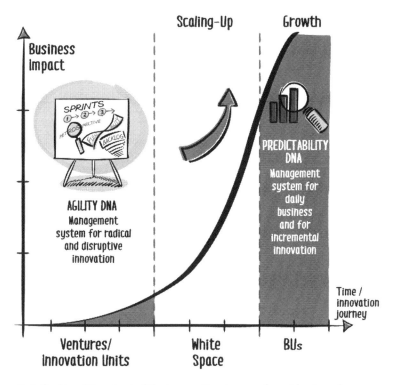

Figure 2-3: Scaling-Up, a part of the innovation journey from idea to scale

The Scaling-Up phase begins when the EBO is "worthy to be scaled" and "ready to be scaled." The phase ends with a sizable business that builds on a newly found repeatable business model. This sizable business is small compared to the corporate mothership, but big enough to run under the same paradigm as Core's by virtue of its size and nature. Consequently, it can be reintegrated or become a new business unit if it should remain within the corporate context. It can also become a stand-alone entity within the corporate group or become a joint venture.

In other words, without success in Scaling-Up, there is no innovation – only "innovation theater" or "happy engineering." And since so many EBOs never reach scale, the business-building problem, in reality, is a Scaling-Up problem.

What are the root causes of the Scaling-Up problem?

The Scaling-Up problem has three root causes. Firstly, two incompatible management systems are supposed to work together. Secondly, during Scaling-Up, the EBO travels from one system to another through a White Space with either an ill-defined or non-existent operating model. Thirdly, one important dimension is missing in the approaches that companies use to structure the innovation journey.

One company, two systems

The first fundamental issue is that for a successful Scaling-Up, two incompatible systems need to work together. This section shows the key points – an in-depth explanation is in chapter 3.

The company's first system comprises Core and small-step, incremental innovation. It is designed to **exploit a proven business model**. **The underlying business context has a lot of knowns.** The company knows what products customers want to buy, the best distribution channels, the revenue model and pricing strategy, how to create and deliver value, how to engage qualified partners and ecosystems, etc. Other market players also understand this business logic – and so the company battles fiercely with known competitors and a known technology base for known customers in a "red ocean."

The associated management system puts efficiency and predictability front and center. Predictability refers to outcomes (e.g., quarterly and annual targets) and the processes that ensure execution. These processes have been tuned over many years to handle individual transactions with high performance, high efficiency, and without mistakes. Under this **Efficiency/ Predictability paradigm**, risk is a bad thing – it needs to be carefully examined and mitigated.

The other system is innovation. It **explores new value pools and business models in a "blue ocean" business context** with few competitors. If this exploration finds a repeatable, profitable business model that captures the value, it may have discovered the germ cell of a sizable, profitable new business. As this business grows, it will eventually be organized under the Efficiency/Predictability paradigm to exploit the newly created business model.

This exploration has many unknowns – for example, customer segments and problems, value potential, proposition, creation and delivery, revenue models, and cost blocks. The optimal strategy for decision-making in an environment with many unknowns is build-test-measure-learn-pivot/move-on[27]. Hence, exploration is not a process but a flow of "disciplined entrepreneurship," and exploration teams need to work under an "**Agility paradigm**" which acknowledges and systematically reduces inherent uncertainties.

The Efficiency/Predictability paradigm and the Agility paradigm are not compatible. If a company assumes that EBOs should reinvent the company while operating on Core's Efficiency/Predictability paradigm – being risk-averse, process-driven, and execution-minded – it will fail. If the company tries to bolt these two systems together, the incompatibility will manifest in "areas of tension" (see chapter 3) that impede a productive collaboration.

The journey through the White Space

The Scaling-Up problem's second root cause is that there is no "innovation infrastructure beyond the lab" in many companies. Such an infrastructure consists of two parts: an organizational home and an operating model. The exploitation of the proven business model has an organizational home: Core's functional organization. It also has a well-defined operating model which builds on the Efficiency/Predictability paradigm. The exploration of new value pools and business models (Playing Field 3) also has an organizational home in the company's innovation centers, Digital labs, incubators, etc., and a defined operating model which builds on the Agility paradigm.

---

27 The Cynefin framework, https://en.wikipedia.org/wiki/Cynefin_framework, provides the scientific explanation

During Scaling-Up, the EBO travels from exploration to exploitation (since a sizable, profitable business needs the Efficiency/Predictability paradigm). But in many companies, this transitional part of the innovation journey has no organizational home, thus obstructing moving along at pace.

Often, the operating model in this part of the innovation journey is also not suitable. **In most companies, Core managers – who have an Efficiency/ Predictability mindset – make the rules and procedures in the White Space** via their role in a Governance Board or by their decision power. However, this is not effective (see chapters 3 and 11). The Agility operating model will not be effective either. The suitable operating model for the White Space is a carefully blended mixture of both.

The fundamental issue of "two systems under one company roof" cannot be resolved; it can only be managed (see chapters 3 and 5). The company needs both systems: one with the Efficiency/Predictability paradigm to win in the day-to-day business and provide the funding for building tomorrow's business. This future business will be conceptualized and validated in the other system with the Agility paradigm.

Contextuality, the forgotten dimension

The third root cause of the Scaling-Up problem is that most companies lack a comprehensive approach to reducing innovation's inherent uncertainties. Every innovation faces four primary types of uncertainty: customer/ market, technical, financial, and organizational. But most companies often only address the first three. They leave out organizational uncertainty, but this is the issue that drags most new business-building opportunities down in a corporate context.

The innovation practitioner calls the first three dimensions desirability, feasibility, and viability. An effective framework that helps companies increase the odds for building a new business needs one more validation dimension that reflects the organizational context. I call it "Contextuality."

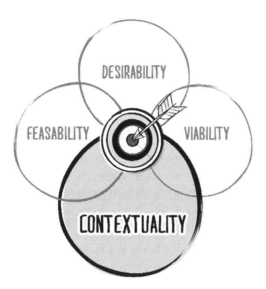

Figure 2-4: Four validation dimensions, including Contextuality, are needed

As I will show in chapter 7, contextuality is present along the whole innovation journey – for instance, in:

- basic validation – why should the company pursue this innovation?

- validating "worth to be scaled" – which corporate assets should be leveraged for an unfair advantage?

- validating "ready to be scaled" – is the innovation and its ties to Core scalable?

- transitioning from validation to Scaling-Up – what is the best pathway to Scaling-Up, and how should the collaboration model between EBO and Core be designed?

- Scaling-Up – how and when should corporate assets be leveraged to accelerate Scaling-Up?

Other causes for the Scaling-Up problem

There are seven more causes for the Scaling-Up problem described below that can be traced back directly or indirectly to the root causes. These issues can – and must – be resolved by any framework that aspires to provide the practitioner with the toolbox to create business impact from innovation.

Chapter 5 outlines the Lean Scaleup, a framework that resolves these issues.

Incompatible governance and KPIs

Governance can be defined as a system that aligns goals, allocates resources, and structures decision-making. Innovation governance usually comprises of "content" (e.g., the scope of innovation and the selected innovation initiatives) and "process" (i.e., approaches, phases, and responsibilities).

Innovation governance is about reducing the inherent uncertainties. In the early stages, the uncertainties are most significant. Typically, innovation teams apply a build-test-measure-learn approach (see chapter 7). Once the innovation has ticked all boxes in the validation scorecard, the team can move it to the next stage. Often, not all of the boxes are ticked, but the team is convinced that the innovation will demonstrate all four validation dimensions – desirability, viability, feasibility, and contextuality – in the subsequent stage. The team can then decide to take the risk and advance the innovation.

Core's governance is designed differently. Here the goal is to ensure the flawless and efficient execution of a proven business model and manage its risks. The governance system of the Core cannot deal with uncertainty. **When it comes to innovation, incremental improvements with calculable risks are the most that Core's governance can accept.** Core's governance system is adverse to radical or disruptive innovations and the "leaps of faith" they require (see chapter 9). Some call this adversity the "corporate antibodies" that eat away the innovation concept as soon as it begins to course through the organization.

Key Performance Indicators (KPIs) are another large area of tension be-tween Core and innovation. Typically, Core's efficiency-oriented KPIs have no intersection with EBO's KPIs – resulting in schizophrenic metrics, con-tradictory leadership objectives, and a translation problem.

Intensive collaboration between EBO and Core during Scaling-Up re-quires the scaleup to have some KPIs aligned with Core's KPIs. This is especially important when the scaleup should be reintegrated into operative business units after Scaling-up. A Consumer Packaged Goods company, for example, requires its EBOs to define some KPIs around the company's retail customers' pain points. With this setup, the EBO solves one big issue: it can easily demonstrate its value by helping Core achieve its own business KPIs.

A different time horizon, a different pace

An EBO's clock works differently than the Core's in two major ways: it has a longer time horizon and yet, at the same time, is running faster in executing the individual activities.

EBO horizons typically stretch out longer than the Core's horizon. In-novations usually need 3-5 years from idea to business impact – and even lon-ger when they build on new-to-the-world technologies or business models. In other words, **the time horizon of an EBO is longer than Core's strategic horizon** – and also longer than the typical tenure of many corporate managers.

So Core and EBO need significant management attention to avoid drift-ing apart. If the plan is to reintegrate the scaled-up business into an operative business unit, a long-term view is necessary regarding issues such as how to embed the scaled-up business, which skills Core should build, which systems need to be docked, etc.

Ironically, scaleups typically run at a frantic pace in their daily activities. An EBO's pace is usually much higher than Core's. This explains the frustra-tion that scaleup leaders have when they see that "it takes Core ages to take baby steps."

The different horizons and pace also show up in complex planning and budgeting processes. Companies usually have formal and rigid planning and budgeting systems that build on defined timeboxes – planning and budgeting for the upcoming year typically occurs around October. When an EBO needs substantial funding for the next phase, it must align with this timebox. The same challenge surfaces when the EBO plans for reintegration into the existing organization. In this case, the EBO not only needs to hit the planning timeframe, but it also needs to align all reintegration tasks with the receiving business unit.

In my view, when Core treats Scaling-Up as a corporate project this is a huge mistake. Corporate projects operate in a defined context with manageable risks – they do not think outside the box of the proven business model. In such a setup, conflicting governance schemes and different time horizons clash hard (see chapter 11). In these setups, one sees the scaleup leaders' energy and drive melt like ice on a hot summer day when they fight against Core's bureaucracy, rules, regulations, security checks, and governance committees.

Scaling-Up requires special people

Success in Scaling-Up requires teams with a different profile than in both the early stages of innovation and Core functions. In the early stages of the innovation journey, emotional intelligence, empathy, and being motivated by abstract thinking are crucial skills. In contrast, Scaling-Up requires people who love to take action, who are more "implementers" than "conceptualizers," and are entrepreneurial and driven by building the new business.

Compared to the Core functions, Scaling-Up teams typically take more responsibility in unclear situations. They have a greater sense of ownership over the whole and not just of parts, are more flexible to changing activity plans, have higher resilience to work in a world of unclear challenges, incomplete answers, and burning the midnight oil to meet milestones.

There is no solid model that can be taught

Scaling-Up has not yet been covered in management literature and management education. When senior managers search for inspiration and guidance in building a new business from innovation, they find bits and pieces, for instance:

- early-stage thinking tools and mindsets (e.g., Design Thinking and Lean Startup)
- structural questions (e.g., ambidextrous organizations, open innovation)
- strategic questions (e.g., disruptive strategies, business model innovation, digital business models, platform strategies)
- technology management-focused programs

To the best of my knowledge, there is no senior management education on building new businesses from idea to scale. Consequently, since there is no clear guidance, senior management's confidence in these questions is limited.

When a lack of guidance and the points mentioned above come together, I speculate that appetite and confidence for business-building drop. Case in point: a study[28] shows that Chief Strategy Officers see initiatives to improve "Run the business" as significant as those to "Change the business" (e.g., disruptive growth outside Core, Digital Transformation). But success confidence in the latter dimension is less than half compared to the former.

Organizational inertia

Structures and processes that large companies design to execute efficiently and predictably on their proven business model obstruct change. Extreme focus on the relentless optimization of the current business model is, on the one hand, a good thing. It helps the company define clear responsibility structures, finetune processes, hardwire them into IT systems, and attract people in line with its mission and culture. But when disruptive business models and different cultures – for instance, Amazon's obsessive customer-centricity – become the market standard, this company is prone to stumble.

This "organizational inertia" was discussed by Harvard professors Henderson and Clark, who introduced the concept of "architectural innovation." In this concept, what matters is not so much whether an innovation is a breakthrough or not, but whether the company's current structures can absorb the innovation and take it to scale, or if the company can morph its entire organization to support a new business model.

---

28 https://www2.deloitte.com/us/en/insights/topics/leadership/chief-strategy-officer-survey.html

Only a few companies align their innovations with their future vision, not with the organization as it currently exists. In many companies, current structures are accepted as given. Trying to fit a new business model into a setup designed for a different purpose makes for an awkward fit, at best. But when the reason to change is not compelling enough, or the company cannot adjust accordingly, innovations will not scale – "corporate antibodies" will eat them for breakfast.

Limited access to corporate assets and the two-front war

I pointed out earlier that, theoretically, corporate startups should be in a better position than VC-backed greenfield startups because they could leverage corporate assets into an "unfair advantage." But the fact that 7 out of 8 corporate startups do not scale tells the story that using those corporate assets is not easy.

The deeper reason lies in the way that these corporate assets are managed. They are sized to support the running business. Functional managers of these assets watch the gates, decide upon resource allocation, and expect to follow pre-defined procedures to request capacities. Their KPIs are in line with the short-term targets of Core; they address operative targets, efficiency goals, and – in the case of support functions – the satisfaction of internal customers. So, in most cases, corporate startups who ask for support are put on the activity deck's long tail.

Two examples illustrate this point. One of the corporate assets is access to customers, controlled by the sales function. The salespeople that I have worked with are very rational people. They are clear on which activities they should spend the last working hour on. And since they have to meet their sales goals, they would rather sell the products and services that pay into their bonuses than spending precious airtime with their clients on promoting innovation (see chapter 10 for ideas on how to overcome this impediment).

Another corporate asset is the in-house expert base in secondary processes such as legal, online marketing, or HR. Innovations often pose new problems for these experts to think through, e.g., crafting a legal framework for a new business model, online promotion of a new value proposition, or recruiting staff with an unfamiliar profile. To solve these new problems, the in-house experts need time – which is often not available since they are already fully booked by the day-to-day business.

In other words, **an EBO fights a two-front war.** One front is in the market where it must find paying customers for its value proposition. The second is internal, where the corporate scaleup has to find its way to leverage corporate assets without being slowed down or even eaten by "corporate antibodies." A greenfield startup could focus its resources – provided it has sufficient funding – on one front only, which is to win market attention and market traction.

No common view on the elephant in the room

In the Hinduistic Rigveda, dated between 1500-1200 BC, there is the quote that "the reality is one, though wise men speak of it variously." This insight might have been the origin of the Indian fable of the six blind men and the elephant.

The fable goes like this: a group of blind men heard that a strange animal, called an elephant, had been brought to town. None of them were aware what it looked like. They said out of curiosity, "we must inspect and know it by touch." When they found the elephant, they groped it. The first person, whose hand landed on the trunk, said, "this being is like a thick snake." For another one whose hand reached its ear, it seemed like a kind of fan. The third man put his hand on the elephant's leg and said that it is like a tree's trunk. The next one who placed his hand upon its side said the elephant "is a wall." Another who felt its tail described it as a rope. The last felt its tusk, stating the elephant is like a spear.

Many companies do not have a common language in discussing how to improve on the business-building problem. They are just becoming aware of the problem, and, since they do not have a common language, their discussions resemble the tale of the blind men and the elephant. So it is not surprising that there is no shared view in many companies, but rather a collection of not-yet-aligned opinions from the major stakeholders.

Typically, senior managers discuss with a focus on the business impact. They see the investments made into innovation, but they also see disappointing results. They do not fully understand the innovation journey, making them wonder whether their company's frameworks are incomplete or not implemented appropriately.

Corporate Innovation and Digital Innovation units also discuss business impact but from a different angle. These departments feel increasing pressure to deliver results, and they want to avoid being seen as an "innovation theater" or "Digital playground." They often have so many options on the table that it is hard to select the ones they should double down on. But quite often, they have no common discussion ground with the operative business since the latter has its eyes firmly on the existing business model and its short-term challenges.

Heads of corporate incubators and accelerators typically have a clearer view of the Scaling-Up problem and the fundamental issues. However, quite often, they do not have the leverage point to reset the discussion with Core about designing an overarching framework for Scaling-Up success. And finally, technology commercialization teams often lack the thinking steps and the language to drive building a new, technology-enabled business.

These are all different views on the Scaling-Up problem, but they describe the same thing.

Why must the Scaling-Up problem be solved?

Scaling-Up is a discipline of its own. The long list of the issues above shows that it is different from both the early stages of innovation and from day-to-day business.

Solving the "Scaling-Up problem" is an essential primary prerequisite for solving the business-building problem. It requires new thinking – for which this book will provide both the tools and the steps – and an additional effort. So why should a company take action to do so? In my view, there are three reasons.

Achieve ROI - Return On Innovation. If a company is not good at Scaling-Up, expected future revenues and financial planning are at risk. As stated above, 85-90 percent of corporate startups fail. In these companies, innovation activities burn money and do not generate sizable revenues – there is no "Return On Innovation."

Succeed in corporate transformation. EBOs deliver a piece of the company's transformation agenda. They are not just a financial play, but also the vehicles to drive transformation. Without excellence in Scaling-Up, the company loses out on the strategic goals and is in danger of becoming irrelevant.

Win in the war for talent. The third reason why companies need to solve their Scaling-Up problem is that success in business-building is essential to recruit and retain top talent. Leading scientists, "rock star" business builders, and outstanding Digital experts are in short supply.

Top talent can choose their work environment. It can start its own company, join a VC-backed startup – or join a large company with its scale and global reach and all the opportunities that come with these.

Studies[29] have found that Millennials – those born between 1980 and 1996, which today already represent 35 percent of the global workforce – are motivated by, of course, payment and financial perspectives. But there are other key motivation drivers as well. Millennials expect:

- being in the best place to work
- creating the best possible products in the relevant area of activity

Companies that fail in innovation are less attractive to top talent. Without top talent, the company falls even more behind. For some companies, this aspect is at the same priority level as the financial aspect or the transformational challenge.

One of my clients is an SVP of bp, the energy giant. I helped him and bp to design bp Launchpad, the company's Scaling-Up factory. He said, "a lot of fantastic people want to come and work in this environment. They are Millennials. I want bp to be able to retain these people, to find the space

---

29 https://www2.deloitte.com/content/dam/Deloitte/global/Documents/About-Deloitte/gx-millenial-survey-2016-exec-summary.pdf

where when they have a brilliant idea, they can take it to scale and be the entrepreneur they want to be – and for bp to get the best benefit from that."

The Scaling-Up problem and the Lean Scaleup

More and more companies are becoming aware that incumbents who cannot build new sizable and profitable businesses repeatedly are at risk of falling behind. **Business-building is no longer an optional way to generate organic growth – it has become essential.**

Fortunately, established companies can use their corporate assets to give new businesses an unfair advantage over greenfield startups. Executives who combine those assets with an "innovation infrastructure beyond the lab" can create a business-building capability that powers organic growth.

This "innovation infrastructure beyond the lab" can be company-specific (see chapter 6), but it builds on three capabilities that are the foundational pieces of the Lean Scaleup framework (see chapter 5):

- Structuring the innovation journey from idea to scale

- Dual leadership (balancing "Optimize the Core" with "Create the New")

- Culture/collaboration of the EBO team both internally and between the EBO team and Core during Scaling-Up

I am perfectly aware that the Lean Scaleup framework is just one cog wheel in the machine of the excellent innovation management system that companies need for innovation leadership. More moving, well-oiled parts are required to have a high-performing innovation engine, for example:

- a clear strategy that corporate innovators understand and use as guardrails for their work – spelling out where to innovate, where to be the first mover/follower, where to be open and where not to be, etc.

- effective portfolio management that ensures proper allocation of resources,

- an effective and efficient organization with clear responsibilities and governance, well-running processes, and massive knowledge sharing,

- open approaches to innovation with the best partners,

- effective management of Intellectual Property

- a culture that aims for "connecting the dots" and making things happen and last but certainly not least

- legitimacy within the company.

So the Lean Scaleup – in particular its methodology part, which is the focus of this book – is an essential part of a company's innovation system. But it is not a one-stop solution for all corporate innovation challenges.

Chapter

03
A COMMON
LANGUAGE

Six essential insights in this chapter.

You will find these again within the text.

 Companies must have a common language for discussing how to solve the business-building/ Scaling-Up problem.

Simply translating the innovation units' language for corporate stakeholders will not work. Core and innovation have their specific professional languages. Hence, any translation will only go so far.

 Companies are simultaneously exploiting the proven, established business model and exploring new business formats or business models. Both are necessary, but they require different strategies to win in their respective business environments.

 Separating Exploit and Explore is mandatory – and most companies are doing this.

The problem arises when integration is required. Examples are service-centered business models, transforming the company, or scaling up an EBO.

 The difference between the "three horizon model" that many companies use and a "Three Playing Fields" setup is subtle but critical. The former has four shortcomings: (1) it leads to ineffective thinking; (2) it does not define operating models; (3) it misses out on considering the interfaces; (4) the timeboxing approach is not valid anymore.

 A corporate startup is not about working in a garage and not about working on a tech product. The race against time, the uncertain environment, and the future growth expectation define a corporate startup.

Therefore, it must trade off certainty for speed and iterate as it moves forwards until it finally discovers a sustainable and profitable business model.

 Scaling-Up is one phase of the end-to-end innovation journey. In the Scaling-Up phase, a scaleup takes a fully validated innovation concept to a sizable business.

Without successful Scaling-Up, there is no innovation – just "happy engineering" and "innovation theater." Without excellence in Scaling-Up, all early-stage innovation is just a costly hobby.

CHAPTER 03

A common language

"We all live in a small unique world.
That's why we need at least one sole common language."

William C. Brown

While a company's business-building challenges are undoubtedly unique, the underlying problem is universal, as the statistics in chapter 2 show. When the business-building stakeholders agree that the company has a business-building problem and want to improve, they need a concise, shared language to structure the thinking process.

This language needs to address the innovation context and the innovation journeys of EBOs[30]. The former is covered in this chapter, the latter in chapters 7-11.

 I think that **a shared language for innovation context and journey is a need-to-have, not a nice-to-have.** Often, the language used in companies is not concise and ineffective. Core and innovation units often find themselves "lost in translation" because every company has two systems under one roof, and these systems are not aligned (see chapter 2).

---

30 "Emerging Business Opportunity" which stands for corporate startup/venture

> **Simply translating the innovation units' language for corporate stakeholders will not work.** Both systems – the one running and optimizing the proven business model and the other searching for a new, repeatable business model – have their specific professional languages. Consequently, any attempt to translate will only go so far. And how should one explain an agile build-test-measure approach to a functional manager who works hard for squeezing 0.1 percent more productivity out of a well-defined process?

Innovation

There is no commonly accepted definition for the word "innovation." In my advisory practice – in non-incremental innovation and building new businesses from innovation – I use an actionable definition that highlights fundamental issues. **Innovation is capturing value from meaningful ideas via new offerings that change the order of things.** I am perfectly aware that other innovation types – for example, management, product system, or brand innovations – require their own specific definition.

This definition highlights five crucial pieces. Firstly, innovation is about **value.** Just coming up with something new is not good enough. "Value" indicates that the innovation has customers who appreciate it and are willing to "pay" for using it. Value is measurable, and this opens the door to install proper metrics along the innovation journey.

Secondly, innovation is about **capturing** value – it is much more than just R&D or invention. It is a journey that is not complete without successful commercialization. History provides many examples on this point. For instance, Thomas Edison and 22 other people invented the light bulb within a few years. But Edison commercialized the invention by developing the "full product" (including power stations, transmission, and metering) and captured the value. Xerox's famous PARC research center is another example. It researched and developed groundbreaking technologies like the graphical user interface for computers, computer graphics, and the Ethernet – but Apple, Adobe, and 3Com captured the value.

Thirdly, innovation does not start with brainstorming ideas but with insights. Insights tell where future value pools will be. **Meaningful ideas** then relate to these insights and the identified value pools. The time it takes for the company to develop and launch the innovation determines how far into the future it needs to look. As Wayne Gretzky – one of the best hockey players of all time – explained his success, "I skate to where the puck is going to be, not where it is."

Fourthly, there might be various **offerings** to capture the value – a new product, a new service, or a new business model may be good ways to solve customer problems at the place "where the puck is going to be."

And finally, the new offerings should **change the order of things**. Another type of "innovation" – incremental innovation – aims to maintain current products' relevance in the current business model via small-step improvements. Companies spend around 70 percent of their "innovation" budget here. But creating a new business that helps to build the company's future is different; it is non-incremental innovation.

Innovation is not a process – it is a flow

Too many companies think that innovation is a process, which consists of a defined input (ideas, human resources, technology, funding, etc.), a clearly defined sequence of steps, and a defined output such as commercial success. Company presentations about how they structure their innovation journeys usually show the word "process" in the title and a linear, value-chain-type process flow.

All experienced corporate innovators know that this is far from the truth, however. **Innovation is not a process; it is a flow of "Disciplined Entrepreneurship."** Every innovation journey starts with many assumptions – about the customer, value proposition, the ability to create and deliver value at cost, the scalability and economic viability of the business model, etc. These assumptions must be validated with a scientific, rigorous approach (see chapters 7-9). But inevitably, not all experiment results will confirm the original assumptions. Then it is time to go a step back, revise them, and run new experiments.

Exploit and Explore

We all know the Swedish furniture and lifestyle company IKEA. It has become famous for relatively inexpensive flat-pack furniture offered in large warehouses outside the city centers and assembled by the customer in their homes, using the provided hex wrench.

Of course, IKEA keeps developing such products. It also works continuously on finetuning and optimizing its global activities. But these days, you also find IKEA conducting activities that are far from what many people know IKEA for.

For instance, just off Oslo's main shopping street, there is a planning studio in which customers can design their new kitchen or bedroom while seeing almost the entire range of materials for cupboard doors, benchtops, or wardrobes.

IKEA also plays an increasing role as a property investor. In Paris' Rue de Rivoli and London's Hammersmith, they have bought prime parts of real estate. Its aim is not just to be a landlord, but also to use real estate to find new ways of "creating meeting points with customers" through new store formats and collaborations with other companies.

IKEA is further pushing to increase the reuse of its furniture through second-hand sales or by renting it out to small businesses or students to counter criticism that the IKEA business model encourages people to buy cheap products and then throw them away.

This example highlights how one company is playing two games at the same time. It is **exploiting** its established business model while simultaneously **exploring** new business formats and even new business models. Both Exploit and Explore are necessary for a company – the first for ensuring today's, and the latter for building tomorrow's success.

Exploit and Explore are two fundamentally different paradigms for moving ahead in two different business environments.

When a company exploits its current business model, it operates in an environment with many knowns:

- It has found product/market fit (see chapters 7-9), i.e., it knows what products customers want to buy

- It has learned the best distribution channel to get the product to the customer

- It has figured out the revenue model that appeals to customers (subscription, license, direct sale, etc.) and how to price the product

- It knows the activities, resources, and partners (manufacturing, supply chain, etc.) and the costs to deliver the product

- It has well-defined approaches that launch small-step product improvements with a good level of certainty concerning the commercial success

In Explore, the company knows none of these. It might not even be clear who the customer for an intended innovation is. When a company explores opportunities for creating a new business, it can do so by following serendipity opportunities or working in defined strategic search fields. **Exploit and Explore require different strategies for decision-making and moving forward**[31].

---

31 The scientific proof is delivered via the Cynefin framework, see https://en.wikipedia.org/wiki/Cynefin_framework

Exploit	Dimension	Explore
Low	Uncertainty	High
Sustain Core	Strategic focus	Build new businesses
Slowly but steadily	Adaptability	Rapidly and fluidly
Efficiency, productivity, predictability	Values	"Create the New" via tech and/or business model
Customer-focused	Customer view	Customer-centric
Safe haven with steady growth	Financial philosophy	VC-style portfolio management, few big winners
Process-driven, 0 mistakes, execution of plans	Culture	Agile, learning at pace, pivot when necessary
Selected and qualified partners	Ecosystem	Known partners, "unusual suspects," startups
Planning, organizing and execution, risk management/elimination, deliver on time and in budget	People and skills	Explorer, recognizing patterns, connecting the dots, feel at ease with uncertainty

Figure 3-1: Exploit versus Explore

The Exploit/Explore dilemma and Digital Transformation

All companies face the same challenge as IKEA. They need to balance running today's business with creating tomorrow's business – in other words, all companies have an **Exploit/Explore dilemma.** And almost all struggle. Studies[32] have shown that only 2 percent of companies are excellent in this respect.

---

32 https://www.bcg.com/publications/2018/2-percent-company

When the pace of change is slow and the current business steady, the "Exploit/Explore dilemma" might not be apparent. But in the case of Digital Transformation[33], the dilemma becomes evident.

If a company takes Digital Transformation seriously, it needs to find a way to maintain profitability in its legacy business while at the same time building new, Digital-enabled businesses. The "Transformer's dilemma" is a tough one: only 17 out of 100 companies can solve it[34].

Ambidexterity

Exploit and Explore must be balanced. Not investing enough in Exploit may result in a successful business, but not a sustainable one; focusing too many resources on Explore at the expense of performance risks disappointing investors. The company must find the delicate balance between the pressure to deliver on short-term financial targets on the one hand while investing in Explore to future-proof the business on the other.

Exploit and Explore must be separated. It is not effective to run innovation with an Exploit approach – and vice versa[35]. But when they are separated, the company can run Exploit and Explore simultaneously, called **ambidexterity**. There are two generic ambidexterity models:

Ambidextrous organization. Initially proposed by Michael Tushman and Charles O'Reilly[36], this model puts Exploit and Explore into different, specialized units. Exploit is located in the Core business and Explore in separated innovation units. Every unit has its specific operating model. The operating model in Exploit is process-driven and tightly governed, whereas Explore's operating model is agile.

---

33 For the sake of simplicity I define Digital Transformation as using Digital technologies in combination with new ways of working for growth (solving unsolved customer problems, Digital products, Digital business models), for improving top line (customer closeness) and bottom line (step-changes in process productivity).

34 https://www.mckinsey.com/business-functions/organization/our-insights/unlocking-success-in-digital-transformations

35 Cynefin framework, see https://en.wikipedia.org/wiki/Cynefin_framework

36 https://journals.sagepub.com/doi/10.2307/41165852

The ambidextrous organization separates Exploit and Explore via structures. This model was implemented first by Thomas Edison, who in the late 19th century launched the world's first industrial research lab in Menlo Park. He recognized the Exploit/Explore dilemma: embedding lab resources into the factory thwarts innovation due to constant pressure to solve production issues. Separating the lab from the factory solves this problem, but this runs the risk of generating an ivory tower. Edison prevented this challenge by leading the lab while at the same time controlling the factory.

Dual operating model. In John Kotter's model[37], Exploit and Explore are pursued within one unit, for example, in a business unit with an integrated innovation function. The idea is that "embedded innovation" aligns much better with the needs of the business. People in this model work on the two operating models mentioned above – switching from one to the other as context requires.

The dual operating model separates Exploit and Explore via the context in which people work. Examples are large, autonomous business divisions with their own innovation units or large IT companies that operate on "Scrum@Scale."

---

37 https://hbr.org/2012/11/accelerate

Both models have advantages, as the following table shows:

Ambidextrous organization	*Dual operating model*
- Independence to "Create the New" – outside the box of the existing technology base and existing business model.	- Avoids the "Not invented here." Smoother transition of innovation concepts into scaleup and an (adjacent) new business.
- Clear link between a company's transformation challenge and initiatives - corporate startups have a clear mission in the transformation context.	- Increased ownership – operative business units own the business today and in the future and do not just oversee today's daily operations.
- Clear separation of innovation and product enhancements – innovation is not at risk to become a "product enhancement workbench."	- Innovation education beyond training. When innovation is part of the business context, the staff is exposed to innovation thinking.
- Clear point-of-contact for the external ecosystem. Co-innovation incumbents, external start-ups, etc. have a defined docking point.	- Supports shift to agile work styles. Staff is continually exposed to ambiguity and iteration, thus inevitably adopts a build-test-measure-learn approach.
- High communication bandwidth between the people working on "outside of the box" issues with "unusual suspects."	- Due to the embedding of innovation, it is easier to continually improve innovation frameworks, behaviors, and toolsets.

Figure 3-2: Two models to solve the Exploit/Explore dilemma

The best ambidexterity model for a company depends on several factors, the proper distance between Exploit and Explore being the first. The ambidextrous organization has a more considerable distance, the dual operating model a smaller one. The figure below shows six more factors that help to select the best-suited ambidexterity model.

Criteria	*Decision support*
- Clock speed and pace of change in the industry (respectively in the industry convergence, see chapter 2)	- When the clock speed and pace of change are high, the ambidextrous organization is better suited
- How far / how fast is the transformation challenge?	- The higher the ambition and the urgency, the more the ambidextrous organization is the way to go
- How high is the company's innovation/transformation maturity?	- The higher the maturity, the more the dual operating model is suited
- Appetite for risk-taking and innovation capabilities	- When a company takes risks and has innovation capabilities, the dual operating model is to be preferred
- Leadership commitment to bridge inherent conflicts between Exploit and Explore	- The higher the commitment, the more the ambidextrous organization might be the best solution

Figure 3-3: Deciding between the two ambidexterity models

As a general rule, the dual operating model is superior if the company operates in a relatively stable business environment. When industry boundaries blur or the company has a massive transformation challenge, the ambidextrous organization is preferable since "thinking outside the box" is more straightforward.

Areas of Tension

Exploit and Explore build on fundamentally different paradigms. Separating these two using one of the two approaches described above is mandatory. But **separation is just one side of the medal – the other side is integration.** The integration issue inevitably comes to the table when corporate assets (see chapter 2) are used for innovations aimed at:

- deploying Digital technology as the backbone of an established business process (e.g., a dairy producer using a Blockchain-solution to reengineer dairy collection and payment with its 4,000 farmers)

- developing service-centered business models (see chapter 2)

- transforming, i.e., building new businesses while intelligently winding down the established business (e.g., my client bp transforming from an oil&gas company to an energy company, or a large meat producer preparing for a business beyond meat)

- scaling up an EBO

Core's Efficiency/Predictability paradigm and innovation's Agility paradigm are not compatible. If a company assumes that EBOs should reinvent the company while operating on Core's paradigm, it will fail. If the company tries to bolt these two paradigms together without any gearbox, the incompatibility will manifest in **"areas of tension"** (see chapter 3) that impede a productive collaboration. Every corporate innovator has seen at least a few of them when they organize the collaboration between Explore and Exploit.

Exploit (Core)	Area of tension	Explore (Innovation)
Existing, proven	Business model	Unknown, not yet proven
Known, certified partner	Ecosystem	Unusual suspects, startups
Top-down, committees	Governance	Lean
Quantitative	Metrics	Qualitative/quantitative
High	Org. complexity	Low
Business metrics	Rewards	Venture metrics
Protection/management	Brand	Might be helpful
I-shaped	People profile	T-shaped
Managers, tenure	Leadership	Founder, identification
Annual plans, Plan vs. Actual	Financial controlling	Milestones, "Burn rate," "runway"

Figure 3-4: Areas of tension between Exploit and Explore

These tensions are inherent due to the fundamental differences between Exploit and Explore. They cannot be eliminated. They can only be managed via a dedicated gearbox with an operating model that blends the Exploit and Explore operating models.

Three Playing Fields

Exploit and Explore can be seen as "Playing Fields" – specific business contexts which require specific operating models. Hard-docking these two to solve integration challenges (see above) will inevitably lead to "areas of tension" in which "corporate antibodies" proliferate.

So how does one solve the integration challenges? The company needs to design a third Playing Field, which also has a dedicated operating model as the other two do. This space stretches the company's technology base and/or business model into adjacencies. I call this space "**Reshaping the Core**[38]." This is the decisive space to win in Digital Transformation and in building a new business from innovation.

The easiest way to explain this is by visualizing the company's activities in a portfolio with business models on the one and technology on the other axis.

On the lower left is today's core business. By going northeast to the top right, one crosses the various innovation Playing Fields. These can be differentiated by how close or far technologies or business models are to today's business. Playing Field 1 contains the day-to-day business and small-step, incremental innovation that aims at keeping today's products relevant. Playing Field 3 is the space with a new technology base and/or a new business model – for instance, an Artificial Intelligence solution that should become the backbone of a business process. Playing Field 2 is made up of innovations adjacent to today's technology base or business model.

Companies who manage Playing Field 2 well solve the Exploit/Explore dilemma. They win in today's business while successfully creating the future business. In Digital Transformation, they see more considerable gains in revenues and earnings[39]. But only a few companies are good at this today. 83 percent of Digital Transformation fail (see above), and 85-90 percent of corporate startups do not make it to scale (see chapter 2).

---

38 I coined this term together with Dr. Ralph-Christian Ohr, www.dual-innovation.net
39 https://www.mckinsey.com/business-functions/mckinsey-digital/our-insights/how-digital-reinventors-are-pulling-away-from-the-pack

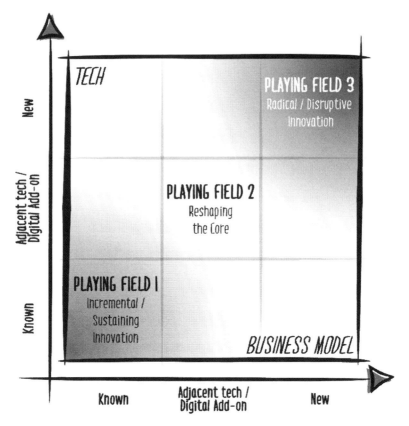

Figure 3-5: Three Playing Fields

Interestingly, these figures coincide. I think there is a deeper reason for it. To win in "Reshaping the Core," operational excellence (Exploit) is not sufficient because there is an innovation element in there, e.g., new-to-the-company technologies or new-to-the-company business models. Innovation excellence (Explore) is not sufficient either, because the ambition of "Re-shape the Core" is to have a sizable, profitable business, which in turn requires operational excellence. **Winning in "Reshaping the Core" – building new businesses repeatedly and succeeding in Digital Transformation – requires a dedicated operating model,** a carefully blended mix of the Explore and the Exploit operating models.

Some companies have a setup that looks pretty similar at first sight: the **"three horizons framework**[40].**"** The three horizons in this framework refer to different time horizons for innovation, and help to structure the innovation activities into three buckets:

- "Horizon 1: Now" (incremental innovation, 1-2 years)

- "Horizon 2: New" (Adjacencies, new customers or markets, 3-5 years)

- "Horizon 3: Next" (new capabilities to take advantage of Digital technologies and/or new business models, more than 5 years).

The difference between such a setup and a "Three Playing Fields" setup is subtle but critical. In my view, **the three horizons model has four significant shortcomings.** It leads to ineffective thinking. It does not have an "operating model" view. It misses out on monitoring initiatives on the interfaces, and the whole time-boxing approach is no longer valid.

Firstly, since language shapes thinking, the "horizon' terminology tends to lead stakeholders into arranging static and distinct buckets, thus ignoring the mandatory integration issue (see above). Secondly, such horizon think-ing does not foresee different operating models for the three "buckets" – in particular the decisive middle ground, which needs to be a careful blend of the operating models for the other "buckets" (see above).

Thirdly, winning in Playing Field 2 requires careful portfolio planning, particularly concerning the number of initiatives. "Reshaping the Core" needs capabilities and resources from Playing Field 1 and Playing Field 3. Hence, if the number of initiatives is not balanced with resource availability, resources are overstretched, and execution time increased.

The fourth reason hinges not on innovation as the previous three, but a changing business environment. In many industries, the timeboxes of the three horizon framework are no longer useful. Technology has advanced to a point where ideas can reach a massive scale much more quickly than in the

---

40 Three horizons framework – See Mehrdad Baghai et al., "The Alchemy of Growth"; McKinsey – See for example https://www.mckinsey.com/business-functions/strategy-and-corporate-finance/our-insights/enduring-ideas-the-three-horizons-of-growth

past. For example, in 2013, VC-backed greenfield startups with a valuation of more than USD 1bn – so-called unicorns – were found in four ecosystems; in 2019, they came from more than 80 ecosystems worldwide[41].

Corporate startups, scaleups, and ventures

A **corporate startup** is a team that companies launch to find a sustainable, profitable, new business model. It operates in the Explore space under conditions of extreme uncertainty and has finite time and resources to find product/market fit (see chapters 7-9) before it runs out of funding and corporate support.

A corporate startup is not about working in a garage, and it is not about working on a tech product. The race against time, the uncertain environment, and the future growth expectation define a corporate startup. Therefore, it trades off certainty for speed, adopts "good enough decision-making," and iterates, pivots (see chapter 9), and learns as it moves forwards until it finally discovers a sustainable and profitable business model.

Corporate startups can emerge from various sources. They can come from explorative innovation units, corporate intrapreneurship programs, or a few people's determined initiatives. Employees are a primary source of innovative growth options – research[42] shows that 70 percent of the most significant innovations in the last century were conceived and developed by employees working within large companies.

Corporate startups differ from VC-backed greenfield startups in two significant ways other than the obvious, i.e., funding source. Firstly, their mission is to deliver a piece of the strategic innovation agenda – but consequently, their degree of freedom to pivot is limited (see chapter 8). Secondly, corporate startups have, in theory, access to many tangible and intangible corporate assets, which could give them an "unfair advantage." However, this

---

41 https://techcrunch.com/2013/11/02/welcome-to-the-unicorn-club/
42 https://kaihan.net/driving-innovation-from-within-book/

unfair advantage is hard to capture in practice and might even be an "unfair disadvantage" (see chapter 2).

If a corporate startup finds such a business model, and the stakeholders decide to invest in creating this business, the corporate startup becomes a **scaleup**. Like corporate startups, scaleups also race against time. They want to build a significant business before VC-backed greenfield startups or other incumbent's EBOs zero in on the business model and take market share. Typically, scaleups have annual growth rates of 150 percent or more (see chapters 10-11).

A company might also decide to make a significant investment into a VC-backed greenfield startup – a **corporate venture** – and then help it achieve scale. When it succeeds, the company profits from additional revenue, the increased value of its share, and the corporate venture's technology.

Scaling-Up

Scaling-Up is one phase of the end-to-end innovation journey, which starts with a meaningful idea and ends with a sizable business. In the Scaling-Up phase, a scaleup takes a fully validated innovation concept to a sizable business. Without Scaling-Up success, there is no innovation, just "innovation theater" and "happy engineering." When a company is not good at Scaling-Up, all early-stage innovation is just a costly hobby.

Scaling-Up can take place in four **pathways**:

– Inside an operative business unit

– Inside the company in a separate function, outside of operative business units (e.g., in a "New Business" business unit)

– Outside the company in a separate legal entity, wholly owned by the company (for example, bp Launchpad[43])

– Outsourced to a third-party "venture builder"

---

43 https://www.itslaunchpad.com

After the Scaling-Up phase, the future growth of the newly created business can play out in four **pathways-to-value**:

- inside a business unit (re-integration of a scaleup)

- inside the company, but outside of the existing business units, e.g., in a newly founded business unit (e.g., a business unit "Digital Solutions")

- outside the company, but still governed by the company (as a separate entity within the corporate group)

- outside the company with limited governance, as part of a joint venture

There are no universal definitions of defining "a sizable business," i.e., the endpoint of Scaling-Up. For example,

- a beverage company considers an innovation to have scaled when it is launched in at least three densely populated markets

- a retailer defines the end of Scaling-Up when the innovation is available at all stores

- a USD 80bn German multinational engineering and technology company set the bar for Scaling-Up success to be "a running, profitable business with at least USD 10m revenue" – because then, "this business shows up in the corporate balance sheet."

Chapter

04
WHY A NEW
APPROACH IS NEEDED

Four essential insights in this chapter.

You will find these again within the text.

 Ineffective thinking tools amplify the problems that arise when a company is not solving its Exploit/Explore dilemma.

Since existing approaches are not sufficient, companies need a new, effective, and proven solution to the business-building problem.

The Lean Scaleup framework is such an approach.

 Many companies' approaches focus only on methodology and on the early stages of the innovation journey.

Thomas Edison once said that innovation is 1 percent inspiration and 99 percent transpiration. If this is true, then companies overly focus on the inspiration part of the equation.

 When the classic validation dimensions from Design Thinking (desirability, viability, and feasibility) are applied with rigor, one can validate "worthy to be scaled" – but only for a greenfield startup.

However, this is not good enough for EBOs since these operate in a corporate context. Consequently, one additional dimension is needed – I call it "Contextuality."

 82 percent of large companies use the Lean Startup. It is not sufficient for structuring the entire innovation journey, from idea to scale. Other approaches are not sufficient either.

While every approach has its merits, none delivers reliable guidance for the end-to-end innovation journey of an EBO.

CHAPTER 04

Why a new approach is needed

"We are working with outdated tools and assumptions."

Rita McGrath

In this chapter, I would like to point out that companies struggle to build new businesses from innovation not only because they do not have a "Reshaping the Core" Playing Field, but also because they use ineffective thinking tools.

Most companies' approaches do not cover the entire innovation journey, from idea to scale. They are **focused on methodology alone and lack leadership and culture/collaboration aspects**. Additionally, the tools are not comprehensive when it comes to validation and **miss out on the corporate context** in which EBOs[44] operate.

 Ineffective thinking tools amplify the problems that arise when a company is not solving its Exploit/Explore dilemma (see chapter 3) appropriately. In my view, companies need a new approach to solve their business-building problem. The Lean Scaleup framework is such an approach.

The following two chapters provide more insight into the Lean Scaleup framework and how companies can benefit from applying it. This chapter aims to highlight that companies need to upgrade their thinking tools. I want to make my point by contrasting the frameworks that I see in many companies with the Lean Scaleup framework.

---

44 "Emerging Business Opportunity" which stands for corporate startup/venture

The latter consists of three parts: methodology, dual leadership, and culture/collaboration (see chapter 5). Furthermore, the Lean Scaleup guides EBOs on their entire innovation journey, from idea to scale:

- **Validating "worthy to be scaled."** Guiding the EBO to deliver the proof points why the company should invest in scaling

- **Validating "ready to be scaled."** Guiding the EBO to provide the evidence that the product is scalable and that an organization can be created that supports hypergrowth with favorable economics

- **Transitioning from validation to Scaling-Up**. Helping the company to work through the activities that create a setup for Scaling-up success

- **Scaling-Up**. Providing the scaleup with a game plan for how to industrialize the product, make the market, and grow the scaleup's organization

Many companies' approaches focus only on methodology and focus on the early stages of the innovation journey. Thomas Edison once said that innovation is 1 percent inspiration and 99 percent transpiration. If this is true, then **companies overly focus on the inspiration part of the equation. As much as this is needed to create new businesses, the transpiration part is often neglected or not done correctly.**

Apart from neglecting the later stages of the innovation journey, current approaches have more severe shortcomings. They do not comprise leadership and culture/collaboration aspects. Their methodology looks only into "worthy to be scaled" and not into the other three issues mentioned above. They do not cover the transition to Scaling-Up and Scaling-Up itself.

But the problems do not stop there. Even in this reduced view, many companies overlook one critical dimension.

Four dimensions to validate "worthy to be scaled"

Design Thinking is an essential tool in the corporate innovator's toolbox. It says that a promising innovation concept needs to tick boxes in three specific areas:

Desirability. Does the concept provide enough value for a defined customer "persona" that they would switch from his current solution to a novel one, take the risk to embed "something new" into existing processes, and pay for its use?

Feasibility. Are there showstoppers that prevent developing a technical solution and taking the innovation to scale?

Viability. Does the underlying business model support a profitable and sustainable business?

If one applies these criteria comprehensively and with rigor, one can validate a good deal of the "worthy to be scaled" piece for a greenfield startup. However, this is not good enough for EBOs since these operate in a corporate context. Consequently, one additional dimension addressing this corporate context is needed – I call it "Contextuality" (see chapter 3).

As shown in chapters 7-11, Contextuality plays a role in the whole innovation journey, from validation to the transition to Scaling-Up and in Scaling-Up. Leaving this criterion increases the probability that Core and the EBO are not aligned.

No reliable approach for corporate startups yet

82 percent of large companies use the Lean Startup[45]. As outlined in chapter 1, this approach is not comprehensive for an EBO. Other approaches are not sufficient either.

Below, the most frequently use are portrayed. While every single approach has its merits, none delivers reliable guidance for the end-to-end innovation journey of an EBO.

---

45 https://www.innovationleader.com/downloadable-documents/lean-startup-in-large-organizations/882.article

Design Thinking

Design Thinking was developed at the end of the 1990s by David Kelley, Stanford professor and founder of the design agency IDEO. It is a systematic approach to solve complex problems with a human-centered focus. Design Thinking is a powerful method to identify customer/market opportunities and conduct customer-centered validation. It also helps to validate the customer aspects of technology-driven innovation.

Design Thinking puts personal interaction between the innovator and the potential customers front and center. It is most effective when three things come together: an empowered and diverse team, flexible workspaces supporting collaborative work, and an agile yet stringent process that consists of six phases:

Understand. In the first phase, the team explore the question of the so-called design challenge. They conduct research and collect relevant aspects of the project and general assumptions and knowledge to develop a collective perspective.

Observe. In the next phase, the team creatively adapt qualitative research methods from social research, ethnology, anthropology, and other fields. they begin to understand the context and the opportunity from the perspective of affected, relevant people.

Define the point of view. The team then synthesize the results and data of the previous steps. They focus on the most promising insights from the research phase and decide who they want to innovate for. They define fictional persons to build a so-called "persona" whose emotional and experienced reality is the basis of the following phase.

Ideate. In the next phase, the team generate numerous ideas.

Prototype. This phase is all about drawing up selected ideas up to a minimum but the necessary detail level. The team manifest their ideas in a physical form. These prototypes help potential customers to understand the core function of the concept.

Test. The team test every prototype with relevant potential users in iterative cycles and collect new feedback each time.

**

Design Thinking is a foundational concept in today's innovation management. It has a broad base of practitioners, and there are academic institutes – notably Stanford's d.school and the Hasso Plattner Institute at Potsdam University – providing education for corporate practitioners.

Design Thinking is not sufficient to guide the innovation journey. It is focused on the early stages and misses out on critical, later-stage aspects of innovation. There is no support on, for instance, how to develop a scalable go-to-market strategy, industrialize the product, or grow the organization during Scaling-Up.

Additionally, I see many companies applying Design Thinking with a heavy skew toward Desirability and little emphasis on Viability and Feasibility. Case in point: in the corporate Design Thinking toolbox of a large company, I found more than 50 individual methods; almost 90 percent of them aimed at Desirability. There were only a few methods for validating Viability and even less for Feasibility and Contextuality.

Google Sprints

Since Google – and respectively, its parent company Alphabet – is frequently named one of the most innovative companies, there is increased attention to how it conducts innovation.

In his book "Sprint," Google Venture's Jake Knapp outlines the process by which his company develops and validates innovation concepts. The Google Sprint process follows the logic of the Design Thinking process but is tightly timeboxed.

**

Since a Google Sprint is a strictly time-boxed Design Thinking process, the same arguments as above hold why this approach is not sufficient for business-building in a corporate context.

Outcome-Driven Innovation / Jobs-to-be-done

Outcome-Driven Innovation (ODI) builds on the premise that people buy products and services "to get jobs done." Usually, there is more than one solution to get a job done. For example, if somebody wants to put a picture on a wall, they could choose a hammer-and-nail solution, a drill-and-wall-plug solution, or use glue.

Like Design Thinking, ODI has a focus on customer needs. ODI adds valuable prioritization methodology, via

— identification of innovation opportunities (by highlighting jobs that are important but poorly served or unimportant but over-served)

— ranking of innovation opportunities (via comparing the importance of the job-to-be-done against customer satisfaction with current solutions)

**

ODI has its strong points when it comes to Desirability and ranking innovation opportunities. However, it provides little guidance on Viability and Feasibility validation. Furthermore, Contextuality is not a part of the ODI framework and ODI does not outline how to scale up validated innovation concepts.

Leanstack

In his two books, "Running Lean" and "Scaling Lean," which are often also referred to as "Leanstack," Ash Maurya added two significant contributions to the Lean Startup. Firstly, he introduced the "**Lean Canvas**" as a tool for developing innovative business models and identifying those parts of the business model that should be validated most intensively. Secondly, he introduced the "**traction**" concept.

He defined traction as "the rate at which a business model captures monetizable value from its users." An EBO can measure traction via metrics that are simultaneously meaningful for both its journey and stakeholders. Hence, traction is a strong indicator of whether the startup will "cross the chasm" from pioneer and early adopter customers to mainstream customers.

**

With the Leanstack (and the embedded Lean Startup), corporate start-ups can address Desirability and Viability. Good traction metrics increase the certainty that the innovation concept will cross the chasm to mainstream customer segments and scale.

Validating Feasibility and Contextuality is not an explicit part of Leanstack. Furthermore, the Leanstack provides only limited guidance on Scaling-Up and how to build new businesses in a corporate context.

Growth Hacking

Recently, Growth Hacking has gained popularity among my clients. It is an approach aiming at broadening the customer base after product/market-fit. Growth Hacking builds on an agile build-test-measure-learn process and emphasizes measuring traction metrics.

The significant contribution of Growth Hacking is that it outlines organizational provisions and tools for scaling up the customer base and revenues after product/market-fit.

**

Growth Hacking is an approach that helps scaleups to make the market. Therefore, Growth Hacking does not guide the early stages of the innovation journey. It does not help with aligning Core and scaleup either. It assumes that the EBO has achieved product/market-fit – but if this is not the case, many resources will go into scaling something that should not be scaled at all (see chapter 8). Growth Hacking supports one of Scaling-Up's four dimensions (see chapters 10-11) – but it is not a comprehensive Scaling-Up framework.

Traction Gap framework

The Traction Gap framework is a relatively new addition to the emerging body of knowledge on building new businesses from innovation. Developed by the Private Equity firm Wildcat Venture Partners, it focuses on the transitional phase between validation and Scaling-Up. In the framework's terminology, this stage starts with "initial product release" (in the Lean Scaleup framework, "Minimum Marketable Product"). It ends with a demonstrated ability to generate traction in the market.

The Traction Gap framework builds on an agile build-test-measure-learn process. Its goal is to show "Minimum Viable Repeatability" (MVR), which is defined by (a) an industrialized product or service, (b) a validated business model, (c) a repeatable and scalable go-to-market approach, and (d) proven traction. At the MVR, the startup has:

- a solid understanding of the overall market (not just pioneer customers)

- some experience in how to acquire customers, including a working product positioning, marketing, lead generation capability, and a reasonable sales pitch

- a few reference customers

- product release repeatability

- implementation success repeatability (i.e., real customers using the product and getting real value)

**

Wildcat Venture Partners developed the Traction Gap framework for their greenfield startup SAAS business-to-consumer investments – not for a corporate context. It is neither designed for the early stages of the innovation journey, nor for validating Feasibility and Scaling-Up. But it provides some guidance on how to structure the critical transitional phase between late-stage validation and early-stage Scaling-Up.

Blitzscaling

Blitzscaling is the title of a 2018 book by Reid Hoffman that examines the drivers behind the exponential growth of selected Internet-based business-to-consumer companies. These companies operate social networks (e.g., Facebook), two-sided marketplaces (LinkedIn, Uber, and Airbnb), e-commerce sites (Amazon), and technology platforms (PayPal).

The book's main point is that a scaleup needs to become the first in achieving a dominant position in a "flywheel market." Then, it can profit over-proportionally from network effects. Achieving this exponential growth – PayPal, for instance, was once growing by 10 percent every day (!) – requires the careful selection of markets, willingness to take extreme risks, and a management style that focuses on growth and action than on structure and detail.

**

Blitzscaling provides many ideas for running the Scaling-Up phase in specific business-to-consumer business models. In other target markets – e.g., business-to-business or OEM-type – its relevance is smaller.

Blitzscaling does not guide the early stages of the innovation journey. It is also much more targeted at greenfield startups than on corporate startups since it does not address Contextuality. And finally, the extreme risk profile necessary to achieve growth will not fit many corporates.

Chapter

05
THE LEAN
SCALEUP
FRAMEWORK

Six essential insights in this chapter.

You will find these again within the text.

 The Lean Scaleup is a framework that helps companies to increase their odds for building new businesses from innovation.

It shows corporate innovators, corporate stakeholders, and EBO leaders what they need to do to validate their concept and then create a sizable, profitable business from it.

 Methodology, dual leadership, and culture/collaboration are the pillars of the framework. They are embedded in every stage of the innovation journey, from idea to scale.

Lean Scaleup splits this journey into two phases that differ by focus, people and capabilities, and the collaboration between Core and innovation.

 Because many mistakes are made before the actual Scaling-Up, the methodology piece starts when there is a meaningful idea.

Applying the Lean Scaleup with rigor prevents scaling something that should not be scaled at all and premature Scaling-Up.

 Quite often, upper ranks and middle management are emotionally detached from innovation. They believe that innovation is essential but do not have high expectations.

On the other hand, there is a lot of confidence – maybe even overconfidence – that the current business will continue to provide sufficient cash flow.

 In many companies, there is an "us and them" between Core and innovation units. Core speaks of "innovation theater," innovation units complain that "Core doesn't get innovation."

These conflicts are not helpful. Leaders build mutual understanding and trust between the two sides. And they find the best solutions for the harsh prioritization reality.

 The scaleup needs to be integrated into Core's planning systems and their associated KPIs so that middle managers and functional experts have a tangible incentive to support the scaleup.

A scaleup needs a growth culture. This culture is performance- and learning-oriented and builds people's capacity and capability.

CHAPTER 05

The Lean Scaleup framework

*"It is very hard to transform
your culture and your workforce
to be a relevant company in the digital world
if all of your processes are stuck in the traditional world."*

Julie Sweet

In chapter 2, I made the point that most companies are doing okay in small-step, incremental innovation but struggle dramatically in building new businesses outside of their core. 85-90 percent of EBOs[46] never scale to a sizable, profitable business. Companies are good at copying past success stories but fail to create new ones.

I also showed that the business-building problem, in essence, is a Scaling-Up problem. Scaling-Up is an integral phase of the innovation journey, which stretches out from idea to scale. Without success in Scaling-Up, there is no success in business-building – and all early-stage innovation is just a costly hobby. Consequently, companies need to pay at least the same amount of attention to Scaling-Up as to the early stages.

Judging by the numbers (see chapter 2), current approaches are not sufficient. They do not provide enough guidance for business-building, and they do not address the problem's root causes (see chapter 4). Consequently, corporate innovators, corporate stakeholders, and leaders of EBOs need a new framework to solve their company's business-building problem.

---

46 "Emerging Business Opportunity" which stands for corporate startup/venture

Such a new business-building framework has to tick five boxes to be meaningful to these groups. It has to:

- be explicitly designed for the corporate context, not adapted from approaches for VC-backed greenfield startups

- be comprehensive concerning the dimensions of business-building and the innovation journey from idea to scale

- have problem/solution-fit, i.e., addressing the root causes of the corporate business-building problem

- be universal, i.e., applying to a wide range of industries

- be field-tested and validated in practice by leading companies

The Lean Scaleup is the first framework that fulfills all these criteria. To the best of my knowledge, it is currently also the only one.

What is the Lean Scaleup framework?

 The Lean Scaleup is a framework that **helps companies to increase their odds for building new businesses from innovation.** It shows corporate innovators, corporate stakeholders, and EBO leaders what they need to do to validate that an innovation concept is "worthy to be scaled" and "ready to be scaled" and then create a sizable, profitable business from it.

The framework provides a concise, non-jargon language to support corporate discussions around business-building. It brings transparency about where an EBO is on its innovation journey, what the next value inflection point will be, and what the activities are to get there – hence, it can also be **a building block for effective portfolio management** (see chapter 9). The framework also helps build the specific **"innovation infrastructure beyond the lab"** (see chapter 6). When the company has such an infrastructure, it can become a serial business builder, thus winning new customers, new revenue streams, and corporate transformation success.

The Lean Scaleup framework encapsulates Best Practices from leading companies and actionable advisory, the Dos and Don'ts in every step of the innovation journey. As bp's Member of the Executive Team, David Eyton, said about the precursor book[47], the Lean Scaleup is "a framework for taking promising new concepts to scale using the best ideas from venture capital and the lean startup world and make these work in a corporate context."

Where does the Lean Scaleup come from?

Like many books in the innovation space, the Lean Scaleup comes from practice. Its origins trace back to 2017/2018 when a "peer group" of more than 20 companies worked on the business-building problem. In several full-day workshops, many videoconferences, and countless 1-on-1 sessions, we worked on the big picture, the key distinctions, and the small but essential details.

The largest participating company was bp. It joined the peer group because it recognized the tremendous, transformational challenge of moving from an oil&gas company to an energy company. Due to the size of its ambition and the time pressure, bp decided to create a "Scaling-Up factory" – bp Launchpad[48] – which builds on the Lean Scaleup's principles.

As the framework's contours became more explicit, I made business-building and the Lean Scaleup the centerpiece of my advisory work. The Lean Scaleup helped a manufacturing company to improve collaboration between its corporate ventures and Core significantly. A Financial Services company redesigned its non-incremental innovation with the Lean Scaleup. And the framework enabled an Aerospace company to restructure the innovation journey.

These are proof points from practice, but there is no scientific study showing that the Lean Scaleup does move the needle when it comes to EBO business impact. There is a growing interest from academia – one case in point is that members from two leading business schools were co-writers of this book. I am confident that we will see academic studies about the framework's effectiveness when more companies apply it.

---

47 https://www.innovation-3.com/scaling-up-book/
48 https://www.itslaunchpad.com

Three pillars and a structured journey

As stated at the beginning of this chapter, many companies' business-building problems are, in essence, a Scaling-Up problem with three root causes: the methodology, or "how-to," is ineffective, leadership support is not sufficient, and the culture/collaboration between Core and the EBO is not productive.

Figure 5-1: The Lean Scaleup framework

 Consequently, these three dimensions are the foundational pillars of the framework. They are embedded in every stage of the innovation journey, from idea to scale. Lean Scaleup splits this journey into two phases that differ by their respective focus, the required people and capabilities, and the specific collaboration between Core and the EBO. These phases are pre-Scaling and Scaling-Up.

Pre-Scaling is about validating that an EBO is "worthy to be scaled" and "ready to be scaled." This validation is done (see chapter 7) along four tracks – customer and value, tech, corporate context, and capabilities and organization – and in three stages: business foundation, business strategy, and business design.

Transition to Scaling-Up is the last stage of pre-Scaling. It is about establishing a "setup for success" in the subsequent **Scaling-Up** phase. In this latter phase, the Lean Scaleup supports scaleups in what matters most: industrializing the product, making the market, growing the organization, and establishing a growth culture.

Methodology

The Lean Scaleup's methodology starts when there is a meaningful idea, not when the company decides to scale up an EBO. As the companies who co-created the framework found out, **many mistakes are made before Scaling-Up** (see chapters 2 and 8). It does not make sense to apply a superb methodology to scale something that should not be scaled up at all. And scaling up prematurely in a corporate context creates turbulence and friction.

Consequently, the Lean Scaleup's methodology supports business-building in four key aspects:
- Validating an EBO as "worthy to be scaled and "ready to be scaled"
- Determining the best pathway to Scaling-Up
- Transitioning from validation to Scaling-Up
- Structuring the Scaling-Up phase

In more detail, these aspects are explained in chapters 7-11. The following section summarizes the main points.

Validating "worthy to be scaled" and "ready to be scaled"

Ideas and concepts are cheap, but Scaling-Up is expensive. Only concepts that are "worthy to be scaled" and "ready to be scaled" should be scaled up.

The Lean Scaleup validation helps determine if the EBO has a solid **business foundation** and a robust **business strategy**. It provides the guardrails for **designing a scalable business** and assesses "ready to be scaled" on the business side. On the technical side, the Lean Scaleup shows **how to advance the product** parallel to the business-related aspects.

Determining the best pathway to Scaling-Up

There are five generic options for the **organizational setup for the Scaling-Up phase**. Corporate startups can scale up inside an existing business unit, inside the company in a specific department (e.g., a "New Business" business unit), in a dedicated "Scaling-Up function" or outside the company, either with own staff or outsourced to a "venture builder."

Depending on the specific situation of the EBO, not all pathways are equally suited. Selecting the path that offers the best chance to generate a large and sustainable new business is a crucial ingredient for Scaling-Up success.

Transitioning from validation to Scaling-Up

After completing the validation of "worthy to be scaled" and "ready to be scaled," the **foundation for Scaling-Up success** has to be established.

The Lean Scaleup helps in working through the issues. Among them are: building an outstanding Scaling-Up team, pressure-test fundamental "ready to be scaled" assumptions, establishing product ownership, and agreeing on the collaboration model between Core and scaleup (see chapter 7).

Structuring Scaling-Up

Turning a corporate startup with a few customers into a multimillion business within a few years means hypergrowth. Of course, it is not possible to anticipate all the activities involved in Scaling-Up. But the better the mission-critical areas are structured, the higher the chance of stability in Scaling-Up and get the most of the collaboration between Core and scaleup.

The Lean Scaleup methodology helps **structure the mission-critical areas**: industrializing the product, making the market, growing the organization, and establishing a growth culture. It also supports defining adequate funding and governance.

Leadership

Leadership in the Lean Scaleup framework is not only about people with job titles that start with a capital C. Leaders are not leaders because people follow them. It is the other way around. People follow leaders because they provide a purpose – a purpose that goes beyond shareholder value and process productivity. A meaningful purpose makes life better for them. For instance, if leaders show them that they future-proof the company.

 Quite often, upper ranks and middle management are emotionally detached from innovation. These companies generally believe that innovation is essential but do not have high expectations that their innovation efforts consistently delivers new business lines. On the other hand, there is a lot of confidence – maybe even overconfidence – that the current business lines will continue to provide sufficient cash flow.

There are clear indicators that **building new businesses will become a critical corporate capability.** Established companies launch new businesses with ever greater frequency. A study[49] has found that 52 percent of companies have "building a new business" among their top-3 priorities. Companies that prioritize business-building grow faster than their peers and respond with greater resilience to volatility and economic shocks.

Building new businesses is a learnable capability. According to this study, companies, as they gain experience building businesses, see more success. They even outperform high-potential startups with a success rate that is three times as high.

---

49 https://www.mckinsey.com/business-functions/mckinsey-digital/our-insights/why-business-building-is-the-new-priority-for-growth

There are four lines of action at a high flight altitude that top ranks and middle managers need to commit emotionally. The second book on the Lean Scaleup, to be published later, will focus on these leadership aspects in detail.

Building the ambidexterity mindset

Past success lures some people into thinking that tomorrow will be pretty much the same as today, and so one finds that corporate strategies are often a forward-projection within the borders of the existing business model. They miss out on threats from blurring industry boundaries, new market entrants, and business model disruptions. They also miss out on the opportunities that might come from a fresh look at how corporate assets could become an unfair advantage in a new business.

The typical senior manager asks if they should focus on making the numbers, often at the expense of the company's future health, or if they should they prioritize longer-term strategies. Almost every time, the first option wins: business is run quarter-to-quarter to the detriment of long-term performance (see chapter 2).

But a growing number of companies say that the decision is not either/ or – it is doing both simultaneously (see ambidexterity, chapter 3). They demand from their management team to **own the business, short-term and long-term.** They require a clear, shared "picture of the future" – where the business model and the operating model need to be in 3 to 5 years. They establish a clear and broadly accepted mandate for **what corporate innovation has to deliver – and which support (funding plus collaboration) it will receive**.

Deciding on the right bets and their growth strategy

Typically, large companies are not short of future bets. They have superior technology at a pre-development stage or stakes in external startups. But often, it is hard to convince senior management to double down on selected bets. Compared to Core optimization initiatives with an almost "certain" pay-back, **the risk/reward ratio of strategic innovation bets is unfavorable** since the arguments for future revenues are all assumption-based.

One cannot prove that the EBO's brilliant idea will be a billion-dollar business in a few years – unless someone else builds it. By then it is probably too late for the company to catch up. Senior management needs to resolve these issues.

The trick is to arrange a portfolio and a sequence of **small bets that eventually build and prove the big ambition**. If, for instance, the company assumes that customer expectations are shifting towards service-centered business models, the best route for the company might be to launch a few corporate startups where each builds "a piece of the puzzle."

The **number of these small bets needs to be limited**. Since every scaleup uses corporate assets, such as functional experts (who usually are absorbed in day-to-day business), a large number of scaleups overstretches capacities and extends the length of the individual innovation journeys.

Besides selecting the right bets, senior management has to make **two strategic decisions in the transitional phase from validation to Scaling-Up**. The first is to **decide if Scaling-Up should initially target building a new business or supporting Core's processes**. Some of the tech-heavy scale-ups that I worked with scaled and matured their technology to benefit Core's operational processes before they went on and created an external business.

The second is to **decide about the nature of the business that the scaleup should build.** This decision ultimately hinges around the anticipated pathway-to-value after Scaling-Up. If the goal is, for example, to

- sell shares of the scaled-up business to a Private Equity firm, the scaleup should target long-running customer contracts with significant margins;

- sell shares to institutional investors with a low-risk profile (e.g., pension funds), the scaleup should target low-risk markets with a "guaranteed" dividend;

- have full ownership over the scaled-up business (as a separate legal entity, a new business unit, or via reintegration into existing business units), then a decision has to be made if the scaleup should target new-to-the company customers or if it should target existing customers to increase the company's share-of-wallet with these.

Creating a supportive environment

 In many companies, there is an **"us and them" mentality between the Core and the innovation units.** Core speaks of "innovation theater" while innovation units complain that "Core doesn't get innovation."These conflicts are not helpful. And when a scaleup becomes trapped between a rock and a hard place, success is in danger.

Leaders build mutual understanding and trust between the two sides. They also engage in a meaningful way. And they find the best solutions for the **harsh prioritization reality,** i.e., splitting precious resources between running today's and building tomorrow's business.

Leading companies have **an effective "ground control."** They make sure that there is constant communication, and that Core helps solve challenges during the venture building mission. I use the term "ground control" because one of my favorite movies – Apollo 13 – provides a metaphor for the ideal connection between an EBO (the spaceship) and Core (NASA). A few people in a tiny capsule, exploring new territory, run into unforeseeable problems – and NASA on the ground with all its resources and constant communication helps them solve the problems and save the mission.

Managing a blend of cultures

As shown in chapter 3, the company needs to manage three Playing Fields simultaneously to own the business, both today and in the future. These Playing Fields have distinctive success factors, operating models, and cultures.

Leaders who understand innovation recognize this. They **nourish and manage a blend of cultures** instead of taking sides. For instance, they encourage the interaction between staff from the various cultures, and they also encourage secondments from Core into scaleups.

Culture/collaboration

Culture is where human beings meet and agree (almost always tacitly) on a distinct organizing framework that provides psychological safety, defines how to be successful, and creates boundaries against human beings from other tribes. Culture often matters way more than strategy. Even if the company has an ambidexterity mindset and applies the Lean Scaleup methodology, it may still fail if it doesn't have the culture dimension right.

Business-building and Scaling-Up require arranging the effective and productive collaboration between two different subcultures (see chapter 3). On the one side is Core's Exploit culture. This culture is based on the paradigms of efficiency and predictability. Annual plans provide the yardsticks for success, and flawless execution is expected.

On the other side is the agile Explore culture of the scaleup. These people have a long-term perspective and, at the same time, a high pace in their daily actions. They are used to revising their plans as they go when they find new evidence about what works. They work in an environment where there are no textbook solutions to the questions they encounter and make their own decisions under uncertainty. Typically, there is a high sense of ownership for the whole in this culture and not just for some parts.

At a high flight altitude, the "culture/collaboration" pillar of the Lean Scaleup framework has four lines of action. The third book on the Lean Scaleup, to be published later, will explain these in more detail.

Aligning Core and scaleup

The "**corporate antibodies**" that eat away innovation are deeply rooted in the KPIs that measure middle managers' and functional experts' performance and shape the culture. These metrics govern Core planning and day-to-day operations, but they do not foster innovation.

The scaleup needs to be integrated into Core's planning systems and their associated KPIs, where it should be on a solid launchpad for Scaling-Up success. This way, middle managers and functional experts have a tangible reason why they should support the scaleup.

I call these systems the **"PM systems"** because they all have a "P" and an "M": portfolio management, performance management, process management, product management, and people management are the most important ones.

This formal alignment is necessary but not sufficient. Additionally, middle managers and functional experts on the one side and the people from the scaleup on the other side need to define the **"partnership balance."** The resulting agreement defines each side's benefits, contributions, and risks during Scaling-up. It should also state how customers profit from the Scaling-Up partnership between Core and the scaleup. Often, the latter aspect is a powerful tool to align both sides.

Creating a productive culture and work style

Often, two cultures clash when Core's middle managers and functional experts meet the scaleup people. On the one side, there is a process- and efficiency-driven culture with predictability and zero mistakes as top values. On the other side, there is an agile, entrepreneurial culture.

Accelerating the Scaling-up journey requires **a psychologically safe space for mixed teams with people from both sides**. This issue is particularly relevant when the scaleup creates conflicts (such as sales channel conflicts or cannibalization effects), builds a new business model, or disrupts the existing one.

Additionally, a productive workstyle needs to be designed and agreed upon as well, as it does not come about by itself. Typically, at the beginning of Scaling-Up, this is a more Sprint-oriented work style, whereas, in later stages, this is a more functionally-driven one with overarching OKRs (Objectives and Key Results).

Managing hypergrowth and create a growth culture

Managing a snowballing business with a Compounded Annual Growth Rate (CAGR) of more than 150 percent is not an easy task. Only a few successful serial entrepreneurs know how to do this. So typically, **scaleup leaders need guidance to master the hypergrowth challenge**. Some fundamental pieces are:

- being clear on what the scaleup needs to achieve to reach the next milestone

- having transparency on the critical (non-financial) KPIs they need to master and the decisive levers

- running a hypergrowth business while at the same time investing in more scalability

- managing in a lean and agile way to advance the whole scaleup at pace, with constant prioritization.

Leaders of scaleups need to create a **growth culture** to support them in the race against time and stakeholders' expectations. A growth culture is performance-oriented – but not a performance culture with winners and losers – and is learning-oriented, but not a learning culture that defines itself by accumulating learning.

In a growth culture, people build their capacity to see through blind spots; they acknowledge insecurities and shortcomings rather than unconsciously act them out. They spend less energy defending their personal value in order to have more power available to create the company spirit and external value. In a growth culture, how people feel – and make other people feel – becomes as important as how much they know (see chapter 11).

Supporting cultural assimilation Core / Innovation

Every corporate scaleup has two functions. The explicit one is to generate business impact. The other, a more subtle one and of secondary priority, is that **the scaleup contributes to transforming the Core's culture**.

When this interface between the company's "Run the business" and "Change the business" parts is functioning well, a virtuous circle can emerge:

more openness and innovation capabilities generate more innovative ideas. These create more openness towards innovation and innovation capabilities.

Heads of Organizational Development, HR, and Digital Transformation in leading companies are aware of this. They organize support for the scaleup – but expect to return the scaleup to support them, as a case in point, in their corporate change agenda.

Chapter

06

HOW TO APPLY
THE LEAN SCALEUP

Four essential insights in this chapter.

You will find these again within the text.

 There are three levels of how to apply the Lean Scaleup framework. They correlate with an increasing organizational commitment to solving the business-building problem.

Level 1 is about cherry-picking and establishing "ground control." Level 2 is about applying the framework to one EBO, and level 3 is about building an "innovation infrastructure beyond the lab."

 In level 1, companies augment their toolbox by picking selected bits and pieces of the Lean Scaleup framework.

Typically, these are validating "worthy/ready to be scaled," transitioning to Scaling-Up and arranging collaboration between Core and scaleup.

Another option is to set up a "ground control" (connector) between Core and innovation.

 Level 2 requires some organizational change in the context of this particular EBO. For applying the Lean Scaleup to one EBO, chapters 5 and 7-11 provide guidance.

It helps to invest in a common understanding of the business-building problem and upgrade the language for discussing it (see chapters 2-3).

 Level 3 is about institutionalizing a gearbox between Core and explorative units to "scale at scale and at pace."

This gearbox, from which all EBOs benefit, could be a corporate function or a dedicated "company builder." – a separate legal entity that actively cooperates with external ecosystems to create new businesses at scale and pace.

CHAPTER 06

How to apply the Lean Scaleup

"Knowing is not enough; we must apply.
Willing is not enough; we must do."

Johan Wolfgang von Goethe

The Lean Scaleup framework shows companies which capabilities they need to focus on building when they want to improve the odds for success in creating new businesses from innovation (see chapter 5). Additionally, it also provides the building blocks for upgrading the company's business-building capability.

 This chapter shows different options. I have clustered real-life advisory cases into three buckets which correlate with an increasing organizational commitment to solving the business-building problem. The higher the commitment level, the higher are its chances of successfully- and repeatedly – creating new businesses.

Level 1: Cherry-picking

Level 1 requires only minimal organizational change. At this level, companies pick bits and pieces from the Lean Scaleup framework and work these into their existing approaches.

Small changes to the current approach

 The Lean Scaleup framework builds on the experiences of more than 20 leading companies from many industries. I think the chances are high that any company will find value in the Lean Scaleup's methodology (see chapters 5 and 7-11) and the culture/collaboration aspects (see chapter 5).

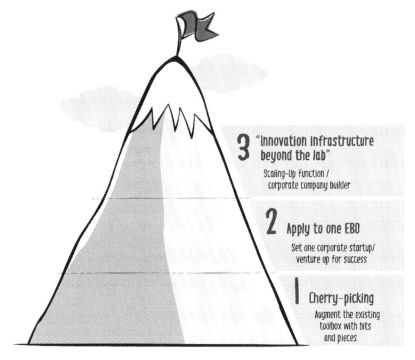

Figure 6-1: Three levels to solve the business-building problem

Typically, companies that operate on level 1 of improving their business-building capability find value in:

- filling in some blanks in the validation of "worthy to be scaled" (see chapter 7)

- applying more rigor in "ready to be scaled" validation (see chapter 7)

- installing a dedicated transition phase between validation and Scaling-Up, as outlined in chapter 7

– arranging collaboration agreements between Core and scaleup (see chapter 5)

Building "ground control"

Chapters 2 and 3 provided a language for discussing the business-building problem, while chapters 7-11 provide an effective language to structure the innovation journey. Some of my clients decided to stick with their existing business-building approach but upgraded their language to discuss issues more concisely and more effectively and installed a communication hub between Core and innovation.

They install a "ground control" (see chapter 5) between Core on the one side and, on the other side, the company's explorative units and EBOs[50]. One person – not a committee – owns ground control to ensure high-bandwidth, fast-paced communication. Hierarchical rank alone should not be the only criterion for selecting this person – they need to be respected by Core people and innovation people at the same time.

To be effective, this person must have direct access to the CEO to resolve tensions. If there is no direct CEO access, ground control will devolve into a passive organization offering advice or, even worse, into a "bad cop" criticizing both sides and resented by all.

Ground control must be on equal footing with senior managers from both sides. It should also have funding to sponsor selected integration activities (but not the whole scaleup phase since this is a company decision). The owner of ground control has five main tasks:

– **Build trust** between Core, innovation, and senior management. Ultimately, trust is essential to mitigate inevitable tensions

– **Develop and maintain high-bandwidth communication** between both sides and a common language that ensures that this feedback is understood and framed correctly from the other side

– Facilitate **translation of KPIs** from one side to the other – in other words, some scaleup KPIs should reflect business KPIs, and business planning should have some scaleup milestones

---

50 "Emerging Business Opportunities" which stands for corporate startups/ventures

- Facilitate the **precise and timely definition of boundary conditions** for the scaleup, e.g., corporate IT systems that need to be connected and cybersecurity norms to be followed

- **Facilitate capability exchange** from the Core into the scaleup – e.g., via a timeboxed secondment – to accelerate the journey and from the scaleup into Core to prepare the transition

- **Organize Core resources to solve EBO issues,** e.g., by mobilizing Core sales resources to reverse a scaleup's slowing sales growth)

To implement the communication bridge, the company should not only define a suitable ground control owner. It should also look at which current EBOs would benefit most from better business connections and serve as test cases for the bridge and who from Core and innovation should initially be connected.

I found that in many cases, **EBO leaders have the most to gain,** and therefore should be the first ones reaching out to business line managers to initiate the dialogue. Initially, an informal communication channel, a "foot-bridge," may even suffice to provide initial improvements.

How to use Lean Scaleup for this ambition

For improving the company's approach to business-building at level 1, it should first benchmark the Lean Scaleup's background, concepts, and language in chapters 2, 3, 7, and 8 against the current setup and then integrate the elements that add value.

Level 2: Apply to one corporate startup/venture

At level 2, the company applies the Lean Scaleup framework in full to one EBO:

- Using the Lean Scaleup methodology (see chapter 7) for validating "worthy to be scaled" and "ready to be scaled"

- Transitioning from validation to Scaling-Up, as described in chapter 7

- Managing the Scaling-Up phase, as described in chapters 10 and 11

- Arranging the leadership support and culture/collaboration pieces, as described in chapter 5

How to use Lean Scaleup for this ambition

Level 2 requires some organizational change in the context of this particular EBO. For applying the Lean Scaleup to one EBO, the framework shown in chapter 5 and the methodology in chapters 7-11 are most relevant. It helps to arrange a common understanding of the business-building problem (see chapter 2) and upgrade the language to discuss it (see chapter 3).

Level 3: "Innovation infrastructure beyond the lab"

Level 3 is about **institutionalizing a gearbox** between Core and explorative units. This gearbox, from which all EBOs benefit, could be a corporate function, but it could also be a separate legal entity – a company builder – that actively cooperates with external ecosystems to create new businesses at scale and pace.

For good reasons (see chapters 2 and 11), both of these should be separate from early-stage innovation on the one side and day-to-day operations on the other side.

Both models require organizational commitment and change. But since business-building is a rather complex issue, any one of these two options should be conceptualized in a "sandbox" first, and then a "Minimum Viable Product" created. This approach ensures two goals simultaneously: it creates a tangible artifact that helps substantial discussions before big decisions, and it establishes credibility by demonstrating, "we walk the innovator's talk."

The Scaling-up function

One of my clients has implemented a Scaling-Up function within the corporate context. This function is hard-docked to the early-stage innovation on the one side, and the running business's functional units on the other side.

In this setup, the company's explorative units are responsible for finding meaningful business model ideas and validating them. Towards the end of validation, the EBO works with experts in business model design and agile methodologies for product development to prepare for Scaling-Up. After this phase, a dedicated function of corporate innovation is responsible for Scaling-Up. This unit reports directly to the CEO.

Generally, such a Scaling-Up function can sit on the innovation side, as in the case of my client, or it could sit in the business function, as one retailer has set it up. Independent of the organizational home, these Scaling-Up teams take the business to an appropriate level so that the operative unit can absorb it.

The answer to the question, "what is the **appropriate level for handing over** the scaleup to the operative unit?" does not depend on revenues alone. It also relates to how much the emerging business has assimilated its management system to Core's Exploit paradigm. In other words, revenues aside, a Scaling-Up function in the corporate context will consider hand-over when it has answers to questions such as:

- Is there a solid understanding of the overall market, including mainstream customers (not just pioneers)?

- Is there a repeatable sales process, including a working product positioning, effective marketing measures, convincing sales materials, and sales statistics?

- Is there a base of reference customers?

- Are the initial products seen as superior solutions?

- Does the scaleup organization have future product release capability?

When the company locates its Scaling-Up function within corporate innovation, it will not improve only business-building. It will also **improve the quality of innovation KPIs**, since there is now a clear differentiation between early-stage and later-stage KPIs.

Such a Scaling-Up function should not build walls between early-stage innovation and Scaling-Up. There are two effective options to prevent new silos. Firstly, conducting a well-structured transition phase (see chapter 7), in which early-stage innovators and the Scaling-Up function collaboratively set the scaleup up for success. Secondly, arrange for job rotation. Seconding early-stage staff into the Scaling-Up unit creates awareness there about Scaling-Up challenges. Seconding Scaling-Up experts into the early-stage teams generally leads to more validation rigor because they have lived through the pain points.

The corporate company builder

When it comes to business-building, what does bp, a Fortune 10 company, have in common with the German-based EUR 950m Beumer Group? They both decided to drive their corporate transformation and professionalize business-building via a wholly-owned company builder outside the company.

Beumer is a 4,500-staff company headquartered in the sleepy German town of Beckum. It is a global leader in "intralogistics" – managing materials and information flow inside a company's factory, fulfillment facility, or distribution center. Beumer's customers run airports, operate manufacturing plants, produce consumer goods, and are leading retailers.

In the past, Beumer was the leading manufacturer of sorting equipment for audio and video disks. However, almost overnight, this business was disrupted by online music. Beumer concluded from this traumatic experience that it needs to go all-in with Digital Transformation.

Beumer's Berlin-based business builder Beam[51] is a crucial lever for achieving this goal. Beam is independent of Beumer concerning decisions, budget, and processes, but there is intensive coordination in terms of scope and direction. Beam's focus is on building new businesses by solving customer problems that are "worth to be solved," not by exploring technological possibilities.

Beam aims to win outstanding, Digital-native entrepreneurs to build a new business together with Beumer's experts. To ensure their long-term motivation, they have significant financial incentives.

---

51 https://www.beamberlin.com/

bp Launchpad is another example of a company builder. In 2017, bp saw that its existing approach to building new business was not good enough to master the corporate transformation from an oil&gas to an energy company. bp's leadership concluded that if the company could not improve its business-building capability, it would only have the M&A option to manage transformation – but this is an expensive and risky route.

In 2018, bp set up bp Launchpad[52], its company builder, as a separate legal entity. bp Launchpad is "a startup, agile environment without the startup chaos where bp takes care of the fundraising and helps the founders to build their business." These are businesses that, from a corporate viewpoint, accelerate corporate transformation.

One of the critical aspects that bp and I designed for bp Launchpad at a fundamental level is to leverage bp's corporate assets extensively. At bp Launchpad, EBOs benefit most from three categories of corporate assets:

- immediate sales opportunities
- live transactional data sets and test environments
- access to a global network of customers, partners, and vendors.

bp Launchpad supports EBOs with a pool of experienced business builders, technology support, and managing secondary processes like recruiting and financial controlling. With this setup, EBO leaders can focus on what matters most: making great products, winning the market, and building an organization that supports hypergrowth.

The two examples of Beumer and bp show that companies who have been through disruption, or fear of being disrupted, have a powerful way to create new businesses that supersede existing ones. Both companies share the view that transformation requires much more than running a corporate incubator that churns through a dozen intrapreneurship projects per year or spending a few millions annually on a few external startups.

The external company builder is, in some aspects, similar to a VC firm: it funds EBOs, builds a portfolio, and looks for successful exits. However, it is much more active in building new businesses than a typical VC firm. In the

---

52 https://www.itslaunchpad.com

view of Beumer and bp, the chances for success in creating a sizable, sustainable business increase when three things are available: leveraging corporate assets, "secondary processes" such as recruiting (see chapter 11) as shared services to all EBOs, and recruiting an exceptional scaleup team.

Compared to the Scaling-Up function mentioned above, such an external company builder offers a few additional, distinctive advantages:

- the option to create attractive incentive schemes for EBO leaders and critical staff outside the company's rigid compensation schemes

- the opportunity of external investments for the company builder or individual EBOs

- a powerful message to top talent that the company builder has the "power of both" (corporate assets plus startup spirit)

How to use Lean Scaleup for this ambition

When a company wants to upgrade its business-building approach, it should familiarize itself with the root causes of the business-building problem (see chapter 2), the Lean Scaleup framework (see chapter 5), and the methodology of the innovation journey (see chapters 7-11).

A common language between early-stage innovators, the Scaling-Up function, the operative business, and Senior Management is pivotal for substantial discussions. I highly recommend that companies that aim for level 3 invest in building a new language. Chapter 3 could be helpful in this respect.

Chapter

07
METHODOLOGY
OUTLINE

Six essential insights in this chapter.

You will find these again within the text.

 The Lean Scaleup methodology toolbox helps companies to prevent frequent mistakes before and during Scaling-Up.

Four warning signs tell companies that they should upgrade their toolbox.

 The success formula for building new businesses from innovation is $S = C * A * L * E$.

S stands for success, C for the corporate context, A for solid and validated assumptions. L is the ability to launch a product and its business model, and E stands for excellence in implementing lean operations during Scaling-Up.

 One key to aligning Core and innovation is to make innovation speak the language of business.

The Lean Scaleup pre-Scaling methodology is a 4x4 matrix. It has four tracks (customer and value, tech, corporate context and business model, capabilities and organization) and four stages (business foundation, strategy and design, and transition to Scaling-Up).

 In the transition to Scaling-Up, eight actions are mandatory.

These are: determining the best pathway-to-Scaling-Up, pressure-testing critical scalability assumptions, ensuring proper governance and funding, building an outstanding execution team, identifying docking points to Core, and establishing the Core/scaleup collaboration model.

 The Lean Scaleup methodology helps manage hypergrowth in Scaling-Up in four areas: how to make the market, industrialize the product, grow the organization without killing the startup spirit, and establish a growth culture.

 The most effective way to manage the complexity of validating "worthy to be scaled" and "ready to be scaled" in a compact timebox is to conduct the validation work in a structured sprint-based approach.

CHAPTER 07

Methodology outline

"Grow with discipline. Balance intuition with rigor.
Innovate the core. Don't embrace the status quo."

Howard Schultz

Applying the Lean Scaleup framework helps to increase the chances of building a new business from innovation. Three capabilities are needed: methodology, dual leadership, and culture/collaboration (see chapter 5). This book's focus is on methodology – the other two capabilities are the focus of two future books.

In the Cambridge dictionary, a **methodology is a system of doing things**. When it comes to building new businesses from innovation, the Lean Scaleup methodology is the toolset or the toolbox. The specific methods or tools provide the "how-to" for handling crucial issues:

- how to validate "worthy to be scaled" in the corporate context,

- how to assess when an EBO is "ready to be scaled,"

- how to transition from validation to Scaling-Up, and

- how to run Scaling-Up.

This chapter provides an overview of the toolbox, from idea to scale. **The following two chapters focus on the pre-Scaling-Up phase** – chapter 8 is about the right mindset to apply these tools, and chapter 9 highlights ten frequent mistakes and Best Practices that I see in my advisory work.

Chapters 10 and 11 focus on the Scaling-up phase. The former is about the "hard factors" – making the market and industrializing the product – whereas the latter is about the "soft factors" – people and culture.

Four warning signs

 The Lean Scaleup toolbox helps to prevent the most common mistakes. When I co-created the Lean Scaleup framework with more than 20 leading companies, we looked into individual tools and specific issues. We also discussed warning signs that signal that the company should upgrade its business-building methodology. We have found four warning signs.

Scaling something that should not be scaled

A famous example of this mistake is Microsoft's Zune portable media player. First launched at the end of 2006, Microsoft discontinued it only five years later. The Zune did not fail because it was a terrible product. The few users enjoyed the interface and audio quality just as much as, if not more, than the iPod. But for the media and the market, the Zune was not a convincing alternative to the iPod.

There are five primary reasons why the Zune failed. If added up, one gets the impression that Zune primarily existed because Microsoft wanted to compete with Apple.

- Incomplete solution for the customer problem. The iPod was much more than a product. In combination with iTunes (see chapter 2), the iPod was a complete solution for solving the customer problem of "manage music for on-the-go."

- Unconvincing product design. The Zune has been joked for its bulky size and brown color. It was called an "underdog alternative to Apple's iPod."

- Bad timing. The first Zune launched five years after the iPod. It came much too late, as the iPod had already rapidly become the go-to device for portable entertainment. Furthermore, only a few months after the product's launch, Apple introduced the iPhone, which combined a software-based iPod with additional functionality.

—   Lack of unique features. Timing can become a secondary issue when a product has features that make it compellingly unique and innovative. However, the Zune was not such a product. Compared to the iPod, it did not have distinctive, superior features, and it did not address any user needs that the iPod lacked.

—   Insufficient marketing. Zune's marketing failed at setting it apart from the iPod in a concrete way. In essence, the marketing campaign said that the Zune was not the iPod.

Premature Scaling

A study[53] on 3,200 greenfield technology startups showed that 70 percent of startups fail because of premature scaling. In the sample of several dozens of EBOs[54] from the companies that co-created the Lean Scaleup framework, we found that this percentage is similar in the corporate context.

The Scaling-Up decision is not only a decision about investing sizable funds to take an innovative concept to scale. It is also a decision about timing. **First-to-market is in many cases not essential, but first-to-product/ market-fit makes a difference** (see chapter 9). When a company wants to validate all assumptions about a new business, it may be too late for a meaningful Scaling-Up. Scaling-Up too early, when there are too many uncertainties, often generates "unforeseeable problems," which lead to sideslips and heated debates about who is to blame.

If one examines the list of the 20 most important reasons why startups fail (see above), proper validation would have eliminated 7 out of these 20. There are understandable reasons why companies are eager to start Scaling-Up. Three pretty frequent reasons are a wrong understanding about product/ market-fit (see chapter 9), senior management's pressure to get moving, or the excitement about the first paying customer.

---

53 https://innovationfootprints.com/wp-content/uploads/2015/07/startup-genome-report-extra-on-premature-scaling.pdf
54 "Emerging Business Opportunities" which stands for corporate startups/ventures

Premature scaleups have not yet ticked all "ready to be scaled" boxes. In most cases, **they have not achieved "product/market-fit" and make typical mistakes** such as:

– Spending too much on customer acquisition (before there is a repeatable and scalable sales approach)

– Overcompensating missing product/market-fit with advertising spend

– Spending too much on the scalability of the product

– Investing development resources into adding nice-to-have features to please early prospects

– Hiring too many people too early

– Over-planning and brute-force execution without feedback loops

Premature Scaling-Up is not only about putting significant funding at risk. It is also about the level of success. 93 percent of premature scaleups never break the USD 100k monthly revenue threshold. Startups that start Scaling-Up after they are actually "ready to be scaled" grow twenty times faster than premature scaleups[55].

A prime example of premature Scaling-Up is the first large-scale attempt to replace petrol-powered cars with electric vehicles. Around 2010, Better Place was a company that developed and sold battery-swapping services for electric vehicles.

The Better Place system combined three innovations. Firstly, it separated electric car sales from their (standardized) batteries; consumers obtained the vehicle and the battery separately. Secondly, it did not require customers to purchase expensive batteries; instead, it offered a subscription-based business model. In this offering, consumers bought driving distance, like mobile telephony contracts in which consumers buy minutes of airtime. Thirdly, it eliminated consumers' range anxiety and public authorities' concerns about infrastructure costs by deploying a network of fully automated battery-swapping stations. In these stations, within two minutes, robots swapped empty batteries with full ones. In other words, the range of Better Place electric

---

55 See footnote 53

vehicles was not limited by the batteries but by the battery-swapping stations' network density.

Better Place filed for bankruptcy in 2013. One of the reasons for failure was that the investments for establishing beachhead markets, running pilots in many countries simultaneously, and developing the battery-swapping infrastructure were way too high.

But most of all, Better Place failed because the public was not yet prepared for electric vehicles. After burning USD 850m of Venture Capital (VC) money, Better Place had only 1,400 customers.

Failing in Scaling-Up

Quirky is a prime example of a startup that seemingly had everything set for success yet failed dramatically in Scaling-Up.

Quirky was a company that took open innovation to the extreme. It made its customers decide which products they wanted, primarily tech gadgets. Industrial designers and manufacturing companies competed to design and produce these products. Quirky then sold the products via its website and through retail channels.

Initially, Quirky did everything right. It had a visionary founder with the perfect background, disrupted the experience of inventing physical consumer products, and won top-tier investors, including Kleiner Perkins and General Electric. It had a board of directors stacked with exceptional people and a wildly engaged community. And it had an outstanding team of functional experts who managed the development, marketing, and sales processes.

But Quirky messed up the Scaling-Up of its business model – and burnt USD 180m along the way. The idea of having a completely open process to product innovation with only a small number of own staff is brilliant. But this idea needs a second thought when one wants to build more than 50 different hardware products annually.

Due to its focus on churning out one product innovation after another, Quirky never iterated its products. For example, the Quirky+GE Aros Air

Conditioner was not perfect. But it had superior features, as can be seen by its reviews on Amazon. The second or third generation would have fixed most of the minor problems, and Aros could have become a sizable business on its own. But instead, Quirky was already focusing on the following product innovations – coffee makers, pet feeders, and 50 other things.

Quirky violated one cardinal rule of successful EBOs: they iterate rapidly to build a product their customers love and solve one customer problem at a time. By doing so, they **ensure that their product finds, maintains and improves product/market fit.**

Ineffective handling of "the big ambition"

In almost all large companies, one finds ideas that potentially could have a massive impact. They could generate substantial revenues, help the company tremendously in its transformation journey (e.g., making a move from a product-based to a service-centered business), and seize pivotal positions in emerging value chains.

But driving these bold ambitions through the innovation journey (if they are indeed "worthy to be scaled") in a corporate context is challenging. Because of their disruptive nature, these initiatives have a high level of uncertainty. They require patience, significant investments, and giant "leaps of faith" (see chapter 8).

However, the core organization will almost always shy away from making these commitments. Instead, senior management often diverts the funds for Scaling-Up into initiatives that either strengthen the Core or build close-to-Core businesses because both strategies have a more predictable reward/risk profile.

These **big ambitions have a low ratio of knowledge to assumptions.** It is almost impossible to "prove" in advance that they will generate substantial revenues and an enormous impact. The only way to provide proof is when another company builds such a business – but at this point, it is often too late for the company to win. An enlightening piece of insight[56]

---

56 https://ssir.org/books/excerpts/entry/a_guide_for_intrapreneurs

provides the facts: 22 out of the 30 most important innovations of the 20th century were conceived in large companies, not by entrepreneurs or academia. But only 5 of these 22 companies scaled their innovations to commercial success.

The right way to approach the "big ambition problem" is to define a strategic roadmap of smaller initiatives that point in the right direction and prove that the individual steps are "worthy to be scaled" and "ready to be scaled," followed by a professional Scaling-Up.

Breaking the big ambition down into a portfolio of smaller risks and investments de-risks the multi-year journey. With this strategy, the individual steps on the roadmap become digestible for the risk-minimizing, predictability/efficiency-focused Core (see chapters 2 and 3) – while at the same time, the first of these initiatives already generate revenues and transformation.

The SCALE formula

The recipe for building a new business from innovation requires four ingredients:

- The business needs to fit with the corporate context.

- The business needs to have a solid foundation – reliable assumptions and not "reasons to believe."

- The EBO needs to be able to launch the product and the business model.

- The company needs to be able to take the business model to scale and generate a lean, hypergrowth business after the initial launch.

When I walk my clients through this thinking, I usually condense the main thoughts into one easy-to-memorize formula. **For building new businesses from innovation, the formula is:**

$$S = C * A * L * E$$

The letters in this formula spell out as follows:

— The **S** is the **success** of the innovation.

— The **C** stands for the **corporate context**. Only when the EBO is firmly embedded in the corporate context, it receives the necessary support – above all, funding and access to corporate assets.

— The **A** stands for a set of reliable **assumptions** about business and technology that have been validated with scientific rigor.

— The **L** represents the ability to drive the development of the technical product and the commercial apparatus to a point where the EBO can successfully **launch** the product and the business model.

— The **E** stands for **excellence in the launched business operations**, including Marketing, Sales, Distribution, Production, Procurement, Supply Chain Management, HR, Controlling, etc.

 Success in building a new business from innovation is the product of the four factors C, A, L, and E. If there is a failure in one of these factors, there will be no success. All these four boxes need to be ticked for an innovation to generate business impact. No part can over-compensate for failure in another one. In particular, **excellence in execution does not over-compensate for having wrong assumptions.**

The Lean Scaleup toolbox supports the entire innovation journey, from a meaningful idea to a sizable and profitable business. The tools to avoid C-failures, A-failures, and L-failures are in this chapter and chapter 9; the tools to prevent E-failures in chapters 10-11. There might still be a failure in the end if, for example, a competitor executes better. But by applying these tools, at least there is an excellent chance to win – whereas, if the assumptions are wrong, there is no chance to win.

C-failures happen, for example, when the new business is not strategically aligned with the company's view on "where to play and how to win" in the future. Another frequent C-failure is when the EBO does not build on corporate assets to create an unfair advantage or when it cannot access these assets during Scaling-Up. **In both cases, the company tries to build a new**

business in the wild – and there is no real reason why the company should be able to outcompete greenfield startups backed by heavy VC-funding or incumbents which leverage their corporate assets wisely.

A-failures happen, for instance, when customers are not interested in the intended innovation. They may know about it, understand it, and believe that it does what it promises reliably and efficiently. They may also be able to find it, try it, or buy it – but they do not care. **When there is an A-failure, all projections about revenues and growth will not materialize** – at least not in the expected order of magnitude. But the converse is also true. If a company competently executes on reliable, validated assumptions that support a sizable and viable business, it is on a stable path to market success.

To avoid **L-failures**, understanding that the EBO needs to build its product and business model simultaneously is fundamental. The latter includes the value proposition, value creation and delivery, and the commercial apparatus that drives these.

I only see a small percentage of products failing in the market because they are poorly built or launched. In other words, they do not fail because of incompetence in designing and building them. They fail because

- the product's value proposition does not fill a significant gap in the market,

- the product does not meet customers' needs in a unique, compelling, and defensible way, or

- the product and its value proposition do not provide enough benefit relative to switching costs or competitor solutions.

Aside from these aspects, L-failures also occur when the marketing, sales, and distribution efforts do not reach the beachhead markets (see chapter 10) with the necessary impact. The product may be the perfect solution to a massive problem, built on reliable and validated assumptions and competently executed. Still, if the EBO cannot get the word or the product out to the target market or if the product is not available, it will fail.

The "E" refers to the end state after Scaling-Up – the end goal, if you will. Chapters 10-11 show that the scaleup needs to move from an iterative, agile validation mode to a process-driven and lean execution mode during the Scaling-Up phase. **E-failures** are, for example, when

- the scaleup is not growing as fast as expected

- it cannot meet the critical KPIs for viability (e.g., reducing customer acquisition costs or manufacturing costs)

- it cannot build lean operational processes

Pre-Scaling-Up: 4 stages, 4 tracks and the 4x4 matrix

The Lean Scaleup toolbox supports the whole innovation journey, from a "meaningful idea" to a sizable and profitable business. It **breaks the entire innovation journey into two pieces, which differ significantly by focus, people, capabilities, and the collaboration between Core and the EBO**: pre-Scaling-Up and Scaling-Up.

The **Pre-Scaling phase has four maturity stages: business foundation, business strategy, business design,** and **transition to Scaling-Up.** In the first three of these four stages, the EBO develops the product and the business model simultaneously with increasing maturity and detail and validate "worthy to be scaled" and "ready to be scaled."

These maturity stages are expressed in business language, not in innovation terminology such as "incubation" or "acceleration." There is a deeper reason for this. The companies that co-created the Lean Scaleup think this approach effectively addresses a regrettable reality: although innovation is high on the corporate agenda (see chapter 2), many stakeholders are emotionally detached. Often, stakeholders do not have high expectations about business-building success. They also have the lurking suspicion that the "innovation guys" are a little fluffy, and their activities do not matter at the end of the day.

One key to getting over this challenge is to make innovation speak the language of business. **Talking in business language – not putting innovation in the foreground but a scalable, commercially successful new business that helps the company win in the future – takes out many frictions between Core and innovation.**

Some of my clients think of these stages as **value inflection points** – points at which the value of the innovation rises significantly (because, for instance, a whole "worthy to be scaled" validation is at hand). Most of my clients link these maturity stages with **funding rounds** – when there is more certainty about the innovation, more significant investments are justified to fund the journey to the next stage.

Transition to Scaling-Up is about arranging the prerequisites for Scaling-Up success. As shown below, activities in this stage are significantly different from activities in the previous pre-Scaling phase. In the subsequent **Scaling-Up phase** (see chapters 10-11), the fully-validated innovation concept is scaled up and turned into a lean, sizable business

The **"what the team needs to develop and validate"** in the Pre-Scaling phase **is organized in four tracks:** customer and value, technology, corporate context and business model, and capabilities and organization.

As a result, the pre-Scaling-Up methodology of the Lean Scaleup is a grid with four tracks and four stages. Every field of the 4x4 matrix contains specific thinking tools that help corporate innovators on their journeys.

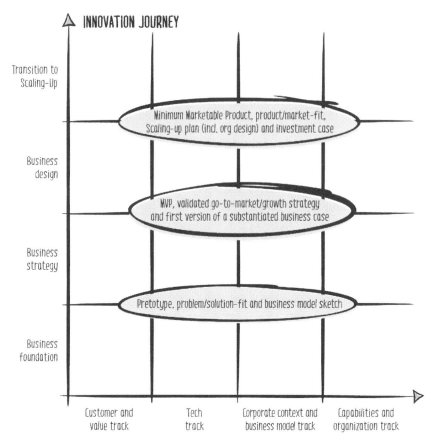

Figure 7-1: Lean Scaleup pre-Scaling methodology – The 4x4 matrix

Some of my clients find this visual helpful because it allows them to sharpen their view on every innovation initiative's status. The detailed view of the tracks and their modules/deliverables (see below) can be the basis for a **scorecard** on the achievements and the challenges ahead – and it can also improve portfolio management (see chapter 9).

Track 1: Customer and value

This track has six modules which are described below. For every bolded item, there are specific thinking tools.

My definition of innovation – "capture value from meaningful ideas via new offerings" – hinges around **value**. There must be a customer who pays for the innovation. This **customer** needs to be identifiable to reach them with an efficient and effective **go-to-market** approach.

The customer's **willingness-to-pay** for the innovation depends on whether or not it solves a pressing problem and whether the benefits outweigh the effort and risks of replacing a working solution. There needs to be a large number of these customers – a **market**. This market's **value potential** has to be big enough and attractive enough to justify the investments for implementing the innovation and creating a sustainable (hence profitable), sizable business.

The innovation needs to have a superior **value proposition** to win in this market. The business that builds on it needs to have **efficient and scalable value creation and value delivery** – which in many cases need **value-enabling ecosystems and platforms**.

In summary, the "Customer and value" track consists of six modules:
- Customer and problem
- Value proposition
- Value creation
- Value delivery and value capture
- Value enablers (ecosystem and platforms)
- Value potential (market size and attractiveness)

Track 2: Technology

The technology track has three modules which are described below. For every bolded item, there are specific thinking tools.

The superior value proposition states how the product (and additional services, if relevant) solves the customer problems, delivers benefits, and explains why the customer should buy the product instead of solutions for the customer's problem offered by competitors.

In the Lean Scaleup toolbox, this product is developed in stages, with frequent customer interactions to check that the customer – and not the EBO (!) – sees the product in its respective development stages to be superior to other solutions. These stages are:

- **Pretotype** (a rapid demonstrator or mock-up) at the end of the business foundation stage

- **Minimum Viable Product** at the end of the business strategy stage

- **Minimum Marketable Product** at the end of the business design stage

Often, the product is **adjacent to other technology**. If it is a physical product, the adjacent technology might be production machinery; if the product is a piece of software, the adjacent technology might be other software that the customer uses.

The superior value proposition rooted in the product should be feasible regarding the existing **Intellectual Property** (IP) landscape and defensible from a legal perspective. A carefully crafted IP strategy that combines targeted patenting, trade secrets, targeted "defensive publications" is a cornerstone for achieving this goal.

In summary, the "Technology" track consists of three modules:
- Product

- Adjacent technology

- Intellectual Property

Track 3: Corporate context and business model

This track has three modules which are described below. For every bolded item, there are specific thinking tools.

EBOs play out in a **corporate context.** Hence, "Contextuality" (see chapter 2) is a critical success factor in building new businesses from innovation. In the Pre-Scaling phase, it is relevant in:

- **solution/company-fit**, i.e., the strategic fit of the innovation with the company's strategy

- **leveraging corporate assets** for an "unfair advantage"

- fit of the innovation with the **corporate portfolio**

- determining the best **pathway-to-Scaling-Up** and **post-Scaling pathway-to-value**

- **branding** (should the scaled-up business have a corporate brand, a corporate sub-brand, or a neutral brand?)

- **funding apparatus**, i.e., the interplay between corporate budgeting and funding cycles with the funding needs of the EBO

- effective **governance**

This track also includes the **business model** and its **financials**. Most validation frameworks put the business model in the context of customer and value validation. However, in my experience, this should be tied to the corporate context for two reasons.

First, Core's commercial apparatus might not be able to handle the intended business model. For example, several EBOs from my corporate clients found out late in their innovation journey that Core's systems – e.g., accounting, financial, contract management, and service level management – could not process monthly payments of a subscription-based business model.

Second, most companies require corporate startups that business cases and financial statements are compatible with Corporate Controlling's thinking and language. For example, when the innovation involves physical products, the balance sheet's implications need to be understood. In the case of a software-as-a-service innovation, corporate controlling typically asks for the **commercial model**'s detailed breakdown.

Scaling up has uncertainties and risks. Hence, the corporate context also involves **risk management**, **legal issues**, and **regulatory issues**. Typically, corporate risk management needs to be aware of these and align them with the risk register. Legal matters become highly relevant when the pathway-to-Scaling-Up or the pathway-to-value after Scaling-Up is outside the company.

In summary, the "Corporate context and business model" track consists of three modules:

- Business model, commercial model, and financials

- Corporate context

- Risk, legal and regulatory issues

Track 4: Capabilities and organization

This track has three modules, which are described below. For every bolded item, there are specific thinking tools.

Building a new business, especially when it is Digital, often needs new **capabilities**. Scaling-Up requires **people** with an entrepreneurial skillset. When people learn entrepreneurship on the job, risks stack up. This should not be the first choice for any company. Digital expertise – Artificial Intelligence/Machine Learning, Blockchain, data science, etc. – is often not readily available in the size that a successful Scaling-Up requires. Hence, pre-Scaling validation requires a hard look into the availability of these new capabilities and how to recruit them.

A new, sizable and profitable business will have an **operating model** and a **scalable, lean organization** that are new and different. In particular, the commercial apparatus needs to be fully scalable to support a hyper-growth scaleup. Before Scaling-Up starts, there needs to be a concept for a scalable organization capable of mastering the intended immense growth rates.

As the scaleup builds a fast-growing organization, the **HSSE** (health, safety, security, and environment) provisions need to be spelled out and implemented – these also need to include **cybersecurity**, which is of paramount importance for software-based new businesses.

In summary, the "Capabilities and organization" track consists of three modules:

- Capabilities and people

- Operating model and organization

- HSSE and cybersecurity

Pre-Scaling: 4 maturity stages

Solving the business-building problem needs to start with a language that puts the business-building into the spotlight, not the product. But the language used in many corporate innovation processes is not effective in aligning core business with innovation units.

One often sees **processes with phases that put product maturity in the spotlight and underexpose business-building.** These processes use terms like "prototype," "MVP," "pilot," and "launch." It is easy to lose sight of the business-building activities and the rigorous validation that the business is "worthy to be scaled" and "ready to be scaled." Another process layout that I often see uses words that are hard to understand for Core's managers and stakeholders – such as "ideation," "incubation," "problem/solution-fit," "acceleration," and "product/market-fit."

The Lean Scaleup framework puts business-building into the spotlight. Therefore, the stages before Scaling-Up express increasing business maturity: business foundation, business strategy, business design, and transition to Scaling-Up.

These stages and their most crucial deliverables are described below. For every bolded item, there are specific thinking tools.

Stage 1: Business foundation

Every sizable and profitable business needs a solid foundation. When building a new business from innovation, this foundation is **problem/**

solution-fit. Problem/solution-fit is about finding a **mission-critical customer problem** and having the initial **proof that an EBO can solve it better than anybody else**. These proofs must be hard, quantitative data coming from **real-life customer experiments** designed and executed with scientific rigor.

The EBO should not stop at problem/solution-fit. It also needs to validate that the **customers will switch** from the existing solution, requiring customers to take efforts, risks, and **willingness-to-pay** to get the innovation.

Most customers cannot make a substantiated call on the value proposition's superiority and their readiness to switch from the existing solution at a conceptual level. Therefore, there need to be tangible, rapid and cheap artifacts of the later product for in-depth discussions. Apart from these so-called **prototypes** and necessary **feasibility checks** ("could we build such a product?"), the product is of low importance at this stage. I advise my clients not to do any engineering at all.

Investing money and human resources into an innovation only makes sense if the market is so big that these investments can generate a significant "Return On Innovation." Consequently, the EBO must conduct an **initial assessment of the market size.** It should particularly look at the part of the market with problem/solution-fit, the so-called **Serviceable Available Market** (SAM).

Validating this value proposition requires holding in-depth customer interviews. These few data points are a strong indicator but not good enough for a reliable business foundation. The value proposition needs to ring a bell with the intended customer group on a broader scale – there needs to be "**message/market-fit**."

If the innovation is successful, it will play out – and probably change – industry value chains and ecosystems. Therefore, the EBO needs to look into the **ecosystems** and an **end-to-end operating model.** In this context, initial concepts on **how to create the value** and **how to deliver the value** and the **scalability** of these concepts need to be validated.

Finally, a reliable business foundation needs to include a basic validation of the corporate context. This validation requires providing the narrative of

why the company should invest in this innovation, an initial alignment with stakeholders on the **business model options**, the **risks,** and a **first rough business case**. The latter requires a validated **market engagement hypothesis** ("with this solution, x% of the market would enter into a monthly subscription of y") to be reliable.

Stage 2: Business strategy

The previous business foundation stage provided data points that the meaningful idea is promising. **The business strategy stage is about two things: creating an MVP** – an early-stage precursor to the intended product that customers see as a superior solution for their problem – and **coming up with a validated winning strategy.** This strategy should outline how to create and deliver the value proposition and grow rapidly to capture the assumed value potential.

Any winning strategy needs to start with an in-depth understanding of the customer. This requires a deep understanding of how customers use existing solutions and how they approach selecting solutions – the customers' **jobs-to-be-done** and the **customer journey**. The search for a winning strategy also needs to include a realistic view of the customer's **willingness to switch** from existing solutions to the innovation. The customer will only switch if:

- the problem has a high priority on the agenda,

- the **switching barriers** are perceived lower than the value-added, or

- when the innovation timing is right.

The latter point has high importance in some industries, such as Automotive. In these industries, there are long innovation cycles. If the innovation does not fit with the window of opportunity between the cycles, it needs to wait until the next one – and this might destroy the business case.

At this stage, a detailed analysis of the **size and attractiveness of the Serviceable Available Market** is mandatory. This analysis needs to look into revenue potentials and the 3-5-year market trends – because this is the time it takes until the innovation creates business impact.

With a 3-to-5-year horizon in mind, the EBO needs to identify the **critical positions to seize** in future industry value chains and ecosystems. These positions – and a **robust IP basis** – will form a defensible position for rapid and sustainable growth. The analysis of future market structure also allows for a clearer view of **make/buy/partner choices in value creation and value delivery**.

Finally, it should design a **1/3/5-years growth strategy**, i.e., an adequate strategy for scaling the business. It needs to clarify what the **beachhead markets** will be and **which markets will come up next.** In this context, a **product vision** that supports the long-term ambition is required as well. In my experience, working through these strategic issues is a surmountable challenge. However, I see few EBOs that rigorously identify the many assumptions behind the growth strategy. Only when these assumptions are validated, the EBO has a solid business strategy.

Combining the insights from the previous thinking steps with business model options allows for developing a **detailed commercial model** and **version 2 of the business case.** The business case needs to be attractive, including the **reward/risk ratio** and a **high-level estimate of Scaling-up investments**, to justify the significant investment into building the business.

The EBO should already make the first look into the new business's future organization. It should develop a **high-level outline of the Scaling-Up organization** and be reasonably sure that it can recruit **this organization's critical skills and resources**. It needs to develop a plan on how to **conduct commercial transactions** (invoices, contracts, etc.) and be reasonably sure that there are **no impediments from HSSE** (health, safety, security, and environmental), **cybersecurity,** the **patent situation,** and **the regulatory situation**.

At the business strategy stage, the corporate context gains importance. Apart from deciding on the attractiveness of the points mentioned above, the stakeholders need to determine if the Serviceable Available Market is **strategically relevant** and **prioritize business model options**.

Stakeholders should also develop a view as to the best **pathway-to-Scaling-Up,** the preferred **options for the phase after Scaling-up** (re-integration, new business unit, separate legal entity, part of a consortium, Joint Venture, etc.), and the **branding-relevant affiliation with the company** (company brand, company sub-brand, or neutral brand). Finally, they should allocate the **relevant corporate assets** needed to create an "unfair advantage" to help in a detailed business design.

In the technical track, one of the deliverables is a **Minimum Viable Product** (MVP). I see many misunderstandings about what an MVP is (see chapter 9). In short, an MVP is primarily a tool to learn as much as possible about product preferences as possible with the least amount of engineering.

Additionally, deliverables from the tech track include an **analysis of adjacent technology** concerning implementation risk, budget, and timeline, a **validated freedom-to-operate** from a patent landscaping, and an **IP strategy** aligned with the strategic issues mentioned above.

Stage 3: Business design

After the business strategy stage, the focus is on **designing a reliable and scalable business that captures the value potential** and **ensuring that first customers use an early version of the product in their environment.** This early version of the product is called a **Minimum Marketable Product** (MMP) – some companies prefer to call it a "pilot product."

While the MVP in the preceding business strategy stage was entirely under the control of the EBO and, for instance, showcased in well-prepared demonstration meetings, the MMP has to demonstrate the technical capabilities of the product in a non-controlled environment (see chapter 9).

The MMP is also a learning tool. Two learning goals are paramount. Firstly, finding out the most appealing features to customers provides essential information for **positioning and market messaging**. Secondly, validating that customers adopt the product with only so much sales and service support as described in the business model, which provides crucial information for the go-to-market strategy and commercial Scaling-Up.

Apart from the MMP, the "tech track" needs to deliver a confirmed freedom-to-operate from a **deep-dive IP** analysis, defined **IP management**, and ensure that the **risks, budgets, and timeline for adjacent technology** are in line with the innovation goals.

The EBO needs to test that the innovation can "cross the chasm" to mainstream customers – otherwise, it will starve, with only a handful of pioneer customers. It needs to **understand majority-segment customers**, their problems, and their expectations regarding a "full product." The **customer journey of majority-segment customers** needs to be validated and investigated if the **value proposition** is also appealing. By doing so, the EBO can avoid the trap of building a technically sophisticated solution for a tiny fraction of the market.

To develop realistic timing in the business case, the **Serviceable Available Market should be segmented** as described above. After that, the EBO needs to work out **a scalable go-to-market strategy.** This should contain operational plans for winning pioneer and early adopter customers and a strategy to win mainstream customers with favorable customer acquisition costs.

Once there are clear signs of **traction** (see chapter 9), the EBO is on solid ground since it has found **product/market-fit**. It should then work actively with its pioneer customers to create case studies, testimonials, joint marketing activities, etc. – because subsequent mainstream customers expect these social proof points.

The deliverables of the "corporate context and business model track" at the business design stage play an essential role in Scaling-Up success. Stakeholders need to start thinking about:

- the value creation/delivery chain's scalability, including **scalability of company-internal units** if they are part of these value chains,

- the **crucial collaboration between Core and scaleup,** the **pathway-to-Scaling-Up** (inside an operative business unit, inside the company but outside of business units, outside the company with company staff or outsourced to a venture builder),

- the **strategic nature of the business** that should be built in Scaling-up (see chapter 5),

- the most promising **pathway-to-value** after Scaling-Up, e.g., re-integration, a separate legal entity within the corporate group, or becoming part of a Joint Venture, and

- **branding** (corporate brand, corporate sub-brand, or a different brand).

These decisions influence how the company perceives and supports the scaleup – but they also affect external talent's inclination to become part of the scaleup story.

In order to make the final decision regarding starting Scaling-Up, corporate stakeholders need a fully-fledged, **detailed business model**, a reliable **business case,** and a **preliminary Scaling-Up budget.** It is helpful to document the main assumptions behind the Scaling-up decisions to support governance during Scaling-Up.

At this stage, the EBO's focus should widen and include "ready to be scaled." The intended business needs an **operating model** and a **lean, scalable organization design**, including a **scalable commercial apparatus**. There should be an idea of who the "**people of the first Scaling-up hour**" should be, the **key profiles** in the intended organization, and a **plan to build up headcount**.

Stage 4: Transition to Scaling-Up

In too many companies, the transition from validation to Scaling-Up is hardly noticeable. The same people who validated the value proposition yesterday are now in charge of taking a promising concept to scale. There is hardly a change in work style and even fewer signs that the relationship between the innovation people and Core has changed.

This is not a good sign. Because success in Scaling-Up, i.e., taking a concept with a few initial customers and a small revenue to a multi-million dollar business in three to five years, requires a very different setup than validation.

From the several dozens of EBOs that were analyzed in the co-creation of the Lean Scaleup framework, **eight mandatory actions in the transition from validation to Scaling-Up** emerged. Cutting short on these activities may lead to an "E-failure" (see above). Although there are validated assumptions for a potential sizable and profitable business and the team managed to develop a Minimum Marketable Product that customers are using, the ultimate result will be disappointing.

Decide on pathways and the nature of the business

There are four pathways for Scaling-Up:
– Option 1: inside an operative business unit

– Option 2: inside the company, but outside of operative business units (e.g., in a "New Business" business unit)

– Option 3: outside the company but with the company staff

– Option 4: outsourced to an external business builder

In the transitional phase from validation to Scaling-Up, stakeholders need to select the best option. Depending on the company-specific situation, some of these four options may not be available. Some of my clients, for instance, have a corporate rule that Scaling-Up has to be in an operative business unit – so the first option is the default option. Other clients do not have a "New Business" business unit, so the second option is not feasible.

If all of these four options are on the table, the **decision criteria for the Scaling-up pathway** should include:
– Level of strategic importance (prioritize option 1 when the strategic fit is high)

– Level of uncertainty and risk (prioritize option 1, when uncertainty and risk are low)

– Amount of synergies in leveraging corporate assets for an unfair advantage and for accelerating the Scaling-Up journey (Prioritize option 1, when synergies are high)

- Level of conflict potential with operative business' channels, customers, etc. (prioritize option 1 when the conflict potential is low)

- Importance of the option to onboard external investors (prioritize option 1, when the option is not relevant)

- Importance of implications and balance sheet and corporate risk implications (prioritize option 1, when the company is prepared to fully absorb these)

- Post-Scaling-Up trajectory (prioritize option 1, when the goal after Scaling-Up is re-integration into an operative business unit)

- Availability of new capabilities (prioritize option 1, when new capabilities, e.g., AI experts or data scientists, are available)

- Does the scaleup's mission pay into the transformation of one or more core businesses? (prioritize option 1, when this is the case)

- Does the scaleup have a corporate brand? (prioritize option 1, when this is the case)

In the context of these considerations, senior management should also develop a first view on the **nature of the business that is to be built** during Scaling-Up (see chapter 5).

Pressure-test "ready to be scaled"

Scaling-Up is expensive – the total budget for a scaleup is easily in the millions. So it is undoubtedly a good idea to **double down on the most critical assumptions on scalability** concerning the product, the intended go-to-market and growth strategies, and the intended organization with its commercial apparatus. The pressure test's goal is not to kill the promising startup that has passed all "worthy to be scaled" validations. It is more about being conscious of what might limit a rapid Scaling-Up, and working these items into the Scaling-Up plan.

For two reasons, it might also be a good idea to include external experts in this validation. Firstly, they provide an unbiased, outside-in view on the status, the question marks, and the open issues. Secondly, the validation team might be biased or longing to "touch the finish line" after a long, arduous journey and thus are more willing to overlook what might seem minor issues that could turn into significant problems.

Develop an initial Scaling-Up plan

Scaling up an EBO is a rough ride. Suppose an EBO that is validated "worthy to be scaled" and "ready to be scaled" has a few initial customers and an initial revenue of USD 500k. If the goal is to develop it into a USD 10m business within three years, this will mean a Compounded Annual Growth Rate (CAGR) of 170 percent.

A good start requires an **initial Scaling-Up plan**. Due to Scaling-Up's dynamic, this plan will not be valid for a long time – but it maintains the momentum and provides a launchpad for the Scaling-up journey. This initial plan also helps establish a realistic Scaling-Up budget and define the Scaling-up milestones essential for Scaling-Up controlling and governance.

Chapters 10-11 provide more insight into Best Practices in how to manage the Scaling-Up phase. The workstreams mentioned there and the issues identified in the pressure test mentioned above should go into such an initial Scaling-Up plan.

Ensure proper governance and an effective funding apparatus

Chapter 2 showed that one fundamental reason companies struggle to build new businesses from innovation is the incompatibility between the paradigms of Core's execution system and the EBO's agile system.

Therefore, the company should avoid treating the scaleup as an established part of the existing business. It is more effective to buffer the scaleup from the parent company's processes and requirements while organizing access to corporate assets to create an unfair advantage and accelerate the Scaling-Up journey.

The scaleup should be a self-contained, relatively autonomous entity, with its own leadership team, governance mechanisms, management practices, and talent environments (including career paths and rewards) – connected with the company via a lean and milestone-based governance. The **governance board** should be as small as possible to ensure high-bandwidth communication and rapid decision-making. It should comprise the key stakeholders relevant for the specific Scaling-Up path and the post-Scaling-Up trajectory.

The scaleup needs to be untethered from the company's planning and budgeting cycles. If this is not done properly, scaleups need to continually compete with core business units for funding – forcing their CEOs to invest a large part of their time fighting for budget instead of doing what matters most: taking the scaleup to scale.

One way of solving this issue is to earmark the entire Scaling-Up budget and release allotments of money when it reaches agreed-upon Scaling-Up milestones.

Build an outstanding execution team

Chapter 2 showed that the people who take a validated EBO to scale need to have different skillsets and mindsets than those who explored and validated the innovation concept. Not everyone from the validation team will have the skills needed for Scaling-Up success.

The Scaling-Up team is ultimately the driver for success. Without an excellent team, the promising EBO that passed all "worthy to be scaled" and "ready to be scaled" validation will not create a new business.

Thus, it is mandatory to build an outstanding Scaling-Up team. It might help recruit domain experts from the target industry who know how to sell into these markets. Excellent interim managers might fill critical positions until the ideal persons are hired.

Some of my clients also have a pool of experienced business builders – "entrepreneurs-in-residence" – who could augment the Scaling-Up team. And finally, entrepreneurial managers from the core organization might see the chance to be part of an existing story and decide to join the scaleup.

Identify docking points to the core company

To some degree, the scaleup will have operational connections to Core. For instance, one of my banking clients requires their scaleups to comply with corporate risk and fraud management procedures; one of my industrial clients demands that their scaleups dock to operational ERP systems. Typically, these connections are not fully detailed – let alone implemented – in the previous pre-Scaling-Up phases. Hence, in the transition to Scaling-Up, these aspects should be **aligned with IT portfolio management**.

These "docking points" need to become a defined work package within the Scaling-Up journey. When the scaleup is re-integrated into an operational business unit after Scaling-Up, this issue is essential. Because then, the whole new business that the scaleup built will be running on corporate systems.

Establish the collaboration model

The collaboration between scaleup and Core stretches out well beyond the docking points mentioned above. In a broader sense, materializing the unfair advantage in the market and accelerating the Scaling-up journey requires a reliable **collaboration model**.

But since Core and scaleup are running on different paradigms, their respective management systems are not compatible by default (see chapters 2 and 3). So **the intended collaboration needs to be arranged.**

Chapter 5 outlined such a collaboration model. It needs to adjust the core company's KPI system so that the scaleup is present. For instance, the sales goals need to include a KPI such as "sell the innovation to 10 more clients" – otherwise, the sales organization has little incentive to support the scaleup. The collaboration model also needs to include a clear definition of the common goals, the contributions from each side, the distribution of rewards and risks, and how the collaboration should manifest at the work rule level.

Figure 7-2: Establish collaboration between Core and scaleup

Establish product ownership

The validation team defined product features and development goals in the preceding validation stages, with only a few people involved. During Scaling-Up, the size of the customer base and the development team is increasing. Additionally, the technical complexity of building a scalable platform with a snowballing number of features and dependencies is also growing.

As described in more detail in chapter 10, **product work in Scaling-Up has four workstreams:**

- Feature work – creating and capturing value by extending the product's functionality

- Growth work – creating and capturing value by accelerating adoption and usage by the beachhead market

- Scaling work – building a platform that ensures that the team can take on new levels of feature, growth, and product/market-fit-expansion work

- Product/market-fit expansion – increasing the ceiling on product/market fit in a non-incremental way by expanding into an adjacent market, adjacent product, or both

Consequently, product development needs to be organized differently in the Scaling-up phase and ownership for the product and the platform established.

Scaling-Up

Chapters 10-11 describe the "how-to" concerning Scaling-Up in more detail. The Lean Scaleup methodology helps to manage hypergrowth in four aspects:

- Making the market; in particular, how to work together with Core's sales force

- Industrialize the product; in particular, how to organize the four types of product work (see above)

- Growing the organization; in particular, how to add structure without killing the startup spirit

- Establishing a growth culture; in particular, how to spot and move the critical levers

Sprinting through pre-Scaling

The most effective way to manage the complexity of validating "worthy to be scaled" and "ready to be scaled" in a compact timebox is to conduct the validation work in a structured, sprint-based approach. This agile way of working builds on small, autonomous sprint teams that aim at fast results to reduce the uncertainties in the tracks, modules, and stages mentioned above.

The validation stages define the topics and the sequence of the sprints. Short-running validation work can already start, while long-running validation pieces are planned. The most critical assumptions should always be of the highest priority because their outcome might decide the future course of action.

Typically, sprint planning aims at work packages that are not bigger than 1-2 days of work. This approach allows for rapid feedback loops and curse correction, if necessary. The various activities with their status and responsibilities are visible for the whole validation team via a sprint board.

The sprint team discusses the status of the work packages in 15-30-minute daily "standups." These standups are not to present results. Outcomes are presented in show-and-tell sessions once per week or at the end of a sprint. Standups provide a forum in which every team member outlines what he/she plans to do today and identifies impediments. By doing so, the whole validation team can "connect the dots," and the team leader can take action to remove the identified blockers.

Chapter

08
THE PRE-SCALING
TEAM AND MINDSET

Six essential insights in this chapter.

You will find these again within the text.

 "A fool with a tool is still a fool," so they say. EBOs can only profit from the Lean Scaleup methodology when they apply it with rigor.

Such a robust, transparent process makes a difference. 47 percent of "serial business builders" have one, but only 25 percent of the less successful business-builders.

 Customer and problem obsession is the significant differentiator between good and bad EBOs.

As Amazon's Jeff Bezos said, "even when they do not yet know it, customers want something better, and your desire to delight customers will drive you to innovate on their behalf."

 Excellent EBOs see relentless validation based on experiments as the primary tool for cutting through the underwood of assumptions, opinions, and options.

They run experiments – many experiments, cheap and fast ones. And then they let the data speak.

 Excellent EBOs are "assumption hunters." They systematically and relentlessly analyze the assumptions which could make or break the innovation they are pursuing.

These teams continuously prioritize what they should validate. They select only the most critical assumptions for validation.

 Successful EBOs want to rapidly get to product/market-fit with a minimum expenditure of resources. In their race against the clock, they continually trade speed against what they can afford to lose for a crucial insight.

This strategy is called the "affordable loss principle."

 Even with the best validation, it is impossible to generate complete clarity and confidence within a reasonable timebox. There will always some unanswered questions and some unknowns.

Consequently, to continue the journey, the EBO and the corporate stakeholders need to make "leaps of faith."

CHAPTER 08

The pre-Scaling team and mindset

"A recipe for a startup that will not make it:
founders have some great idea they know everyone is going to love,
and that's what they're going to build, no matter what."

Paul Abraham

When companies venture beyond their core business, the failure rate increases dramatically (see chapter 2). When EBOs[57] use the validation tools outlined in chapter 7 with rigor, they validate if the business idea is "worthy to be scaled" and "ready to be scaled." When these two cannot be validated, and there is no meaningful pivot (see chapter 9), there is no reason to spend precious financial and human resources on Scaling-up.

The crucial word is rigor. "A fool with a tool is still a fool," so they say. When an EBO does not use the tools in the 4x4 validation grid (see chapter 7) with the right mindset, it will draw wrong conclusions and make bad decisions.

But the converse is also true: **when an EBO team uses these tools with the right mindset, it has a robust, transparent process from idea to scale. Such a process makes a difference.** 47 percent of companies that are "serial business builders" have one, but only 25 percent of those companies who are less successful in building new businesses[58].

---

57 "Emerging Business Opportunities" which stands for corporate startups/ventures
58 https://www.mckinsey.com/business-functions/mckinsey-digital/our-insights/why-business-building-is-the-new-priority-for-growth

Any startup's goal is to find a new, repeatable, and profitable business model. This requires understanding what to build and for who. But here is the sad story: the top two reasons why (greenfield) startups fail[59] are "no market need" and "ran out of cash." These two are closely related. If a startup builds a product that the market does not need, it will not generate sales and run out of cash. So, to put it bluntly, **most startups fail because they build something nobody wants.**

Underperforming EBOs think they know what their customers want because they have an almost prophetic "vision." They raise money by presenting ideas full of world-changing feature ideas and buzzwords like "Artificial Intelligence," "Blockchain," or "Quantum Computing."

One of the first things they do is hire a team. Then the team locks themselves in to "crack the code." They spend more time preparing the MVP (so they say) than talking to customers. When they reappear from their engineering work, this so-called MVP is frankly not an MVP anymore – it is full of more or less relevant features. They then go out and try to convince customers about the product and their stakeholders about more funding because "the breakthrough seems imminent."

These EBOs, who raise substantial money without validating their idea first, are like traders who pick stocks randomly. They may win out of luck. But in most instances, they fail.

Team qualities of excellent corporate startups/ventures

Excellent EBOs are passionate and obsessed about customers and a problem "worth to be solved." They do not push a specific technology just because it is the hot new thing. They do not confuse a stringent thinking process – such as the Lean Scaleup – with filling out templates.

With scientific rigor and a high sense of urgency, they try to find a repeatable, scalable business model. They map out and prioritize their

---

59 https://fortune.com/2014/09/25/why-startups-fail-according-to-their-founders/

assumptions, conduct meaningful experiments, let the data speak, draw conclusions from the data and move on.

Customer obsession

Excellent EBOs want to understand the problem they desire to solve deeper than the customer does. They know that it is not only about the problem. The problem context and how the customer makes decisions about potential solutions are equally important. They talk to their customers:

- before building,

- while they are building (an MVP or a Minimum Marketable Product), and

- after they have built.

 Customer and problem obsession is the significant differentiator between good and bad EBOs. As Amazon's Jeff Bezos said, "even when they do not yet know it, customers want something better, and your desire to delight customers will drive you to innovate on their behalf."[60]

Excellent EBOs have a high percentage of customer-obsessed people, even in technical functions. I find it very stimulating to hear a founder speaking with great passion about potential customers, their problems and their context, and how the EBO plans to succeed. Nothing beats the feeling when it all clicks. The buzz from those conversations has fueled many late-night discussions as I sought to understand further the team's vision.

Data-driven

There are many assumptions when a company launches an EBO to find a scalable and profitable business model. These assumptions concern all validation tracks mentioned in chapter 7 – customer and value, technology, corporate context and business model, and capabilities and organization. **Excellent EBOs are not only customer-obsessed; they are also data-driven.**

---

60 Jeff Bezos, 2016 letter to shareholders

They see relentless validation based on experiments as the primary tool for cutting through the underwood of assumptions, opinions, and options. One EBO leader said to me, **"I am not the master decision-maker. We run experiments. Many experiments, cheap and fast ones. And then we let the data speak."**

This data provides the hard facts that the EBO needs to lead the internal discussions, especially when it tells a story that contradicts the stakeholders' initial expectations.

I think that corporate stakeholders should insist more on experimentation and data. It is not only about innovation; it is also about Core. Every insight that the EBO collects in innovation interviews might also be relevant for the core organization's sales, marketing, business development, and corporate strategy departments. **In my view, this is enormous and untapped potential in many companies.**

Sense of urgency, focus on the goals

EBOs are in a constant race against time. They need to reach product/market-fit before they run out of corporate funding and support, and they have to do so more quickly than the company's competitors or VC-backed greenfield startups. In excellent EBOs, I observe a high sense of urgency. I feel the **desire of all team members to make every single day count**.

In excellent EBOs, the team members also manage a delicate balance between urgency and patience. They know when they should move slowly so that they can progress rapidly. For instance, when the EBO team works together with Core – who generally are running at a lower clock speed – they are well-advised to adapt. The art is to keep a high pace without becoming hectic and develop tunnel vision.

Before Scaling-Up, any successful EBO has two main goals: it needs to show that the innovation is "worthy to be scaled" and "ready to be scaled" (see chapter 7). However, **teams can be distracted from their primary goals**. And indeed, some of these distractions may be essential for survival. For instance, when the corporate environment is not supportive (see chapter 5, "dual leadership" and "culture/collaboration"), the team needs to fight for funding and manage corporate politics constantly. Some EBO leaders told me that they spend 25 percent of their time on these activities.

The EBO can also be distracted when it spends significant time serving as an external or internal showcase for innovation. And finally, there are self-made distractions, like participating in founder events, in business plan competitions, or in expert panels that rarely provide any benefit but eat up a lot of time.

Validation awareness

Excellent EBOs are "assumption hunters." They systematically and relentlessly analyze the assumptions (see above). They are aware that these assumptions could make or break the innovation they are pursuing.

These teams continuously prioritize what they should validate. Since the team has a sense of urgency, they select only the most critical assumptions for validation. Excellent EBOs are aware that there might be success-relevant issues they do not know yet – the "unknown unknowns." They run cheap and fast probing experiments to probe this space.

Insight-driven, not process-driven

Processes, including validation processes, are essential because they help operate effectively and efficiently and deliver quality predictably. But if one is not watchful, the process can become the main thing. When the process becomes more important than the content, the EBO team shifts its attention from validating with scientific rigor to ticking all the boxes they are supposed to tick.

Sometimes teams take shortcuts. To tick the box labeled "customer discovery and problem understanding," they rely on market research and surveys. While valuable, these inputs are not a substitute for spending time with customers. Studying and understanding customer stories delivers more insights than averages in surveys (see chapter 9).

Working on the "affordable loss principle"

 Successful EBOs want to rapidly get to product/market-fit with a minimum expenditure of resources. **In their race against the clock, they continually trade speed against what they can afford to lose** (avoiding all-or-nothing activities, of course) **for a crucial insight. This strategy is called the "affordable loss principle."**

This principle is suitable for the explorative space in which the EBO operates but not for Core (see chapters 2-3). For example, market research in Core builds on in-depth quantitative studies. From these studies' results, marketing/sales managers delineate the target market and the go-to-market strategy. Excellent EBOs conduct traditional market research only to a certain point. Their market research comes implicitly from their innovation interviews.

Excellent EBOs are well-familiar with market research and strategy. But **they do not tie themselves to a theoretical or pre-conceived "market" or "strategic" construct**. They are open to segmenting the market by value proposition or creating new markets that have not been defined yet.

Agility

Chapter 7 showed that the pre-Scaling validation of "worthy to be scaled" and "ready to be scaled" is multi-dimensional. The validation journey is not linear and straightforward. There are many uncertainties, and not every assumption will stand the reality check – which will send the team back one step to revise assumptions.

Agile work styles are effective in solving these challenges. At a high level, the fundamentals are simple. The EBO is empowered to plan their work and make decisions. The "product owner" – typically the corporate sponsor or a senior manager from an operative business unit – helps the team to continuously (and ruthlessly) prioritize the list of open issues and untested assumptions.

The team breaks down the tasks into daily deliverables that fill up a "Sprint," which delivers an increment to the innovation journey. The team members update themselves in daily standups on the individual pieces of work and the progress. In Sprint reviews, the team inspects the delivered increment, and in Sprint retrospectives, the team inspects and improves itself.

Learning at pace

On top of the qualities mentioned above, excellent EBOs learn quicker and more deliberately than others. "Learning at pace" refers to:

- the context of the innovation – for instance, the underlying Digital technology,

- what the team has learned from things that did not work out as planned (fail fast, fail forward), and

- effective thinking models, experiences from other companies, insights about innovation's nature, and behaviors and processes that improve teamwork.

I have had the pleasure of working with excellent EBOs that are learning at pace. Often, this learning builds on two pillars: absorbing impulses from other people and rapid double feedback loops.

For the former, "lunch and learn" sessions with free food, a talk on the side, and a discussion afterward or evening sessions with some pretzels and beverages might be options. Some of these sessions may even be "open house" within the company, helping the team promote its work and disseminate the innovation message.

Rapid double feedback loops involve team-external experts from inside the company or from a pool of trusted advisors. **They help the innovation team understand what they need to learn** and are much more than a "Sprint retrospective" in which the team analyzes its most recent work. Rapid double feedback loops go deeper. They look at the root causes of difficulties and challenges – and quite often, they unearth "unknown unknowns" in time so that they do not become challenges in the future.

Courage and perseverance

EBOs explore the space outside of the core business. They are operating in uncharted territory and trying to find a repeatable, scalable and profitable business model. However, most good ideas are controversial before they become apparent. Typically, ideas that change the order of things are not welcome across the board. They encounter skepticism, sometimes even sarcasm, and the usual "we have never done this before."

It takes courage to accept being misunderstood for a long time without becoming stubborn and to defend a big idea over a long time while being aware that it might turn out not to be big after all. And with big ideas, there is more than one debate to stand. It takes perseverance and storytelling skills (see below) to lead and win the arguments over and over again.

Members of EBOs that raise the bar are also courageous action-takers. **Their attitude is "I find a way or I make one," and they would rather ask for forgiveness for their actions than for permission.** They do not see the point in an endless exchange of arguments. Instead, these members are taking action to collect indisputable proof points.

Curiosity

Outstanding EBO teams are curious by nature. They go way beyond what is needed – they apply headroom thinking and explore what is possible.

I think the best methodology for profoundly understanding customers is not a methodology at all, but curiosity. **I advise my EBO clients to stay curious.** They should work on the customer's premises (if this is possible), read the magazines their customers read, listen to webinars that their customers attend, join their customer's trade associations and professional networks, etc. By their example, the most curious team members typically inspire the whole team to emerge in the customer context.

Curiosity also shows up in lively debates within the EBO. Outstanding members from EBO teams do not simply ask "what?", "what if?" and "what else?". Their curiosity leads them to understand the details to make more and better decisions in the future.

Of course, challenging people seriously and constructively without discouraging them requires social skills and a good sense of balance – but it is worth it. I witnessed several light bulb moments when the crucial insight did not show up in the bright spotlight but in the argument's subtle shades.

Leaps of faith

When EBOs do not validate the innovation in the early stages of the journey, they risk losing time and money. Along the journey, proper validation increases clarity (for example, on the best business model, the most effective growth strategy, and the scalability of partners in the value chain) and building confidence (by reducing uncertainty).

In theory, clarity and confidence should increase continuously along with the validation (see the validation stages in chapter 7). There should be a point where clarity and confidence are so high that further investments are fully justified. This is visualized on the left-hand side of the figure below.

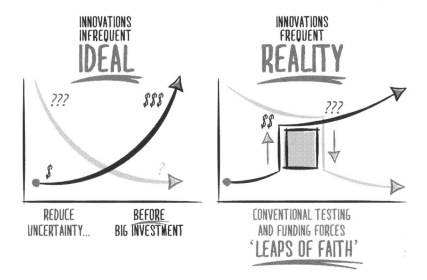

Figure 8-1: "Leaps of faith"

 However, even with the best validation, it is impossible to generate complete clarity and confidence within a reasonable timebox. There will always some unanswered questions and some unknowns.

Consequently, to continue the journey, the EBO and the corporate stakeholders need to make "leaps of faith" (see the right-hand side of the figure above).

There is no point in denying this reality. The question is much more what the best strategies are in this context. I advise my clients that the EBO should consider three things:

– Focus on the "questions and unknowns" zone (the shaded area in the figure above) and not on getting more profound insights into what the team has already validated.

– Map out the most critical assumptions before making the leap of faith. These assumptions can be monitored, providing more certainty or early warning signs that the EBO is on the wrong track.

– Apply the "affordable loss principle." Few decisions are not reversible, and so the question should be not what the company is willing to invest but rather what the company could afford to lose.

Storytelling

An EBO has to explain its ambition so often that all team members should acquire the skill of telling its story in an inspiring and professional way. However, only a few EBOs train themselves to get their story across to various audiences.

Storytelling is emotional. The storyteller tries to win the hearts of the audience by crafting visual and engaging images. Of course, this statement is not downplaying quantitative data and hard facts. But I observed so many times – especially in discussions between the EBO and Core – that **a shared picture makes it so much easier to build bridges and align.**

Not everybody is a good storyteller. Typically, engineers are not so much into storytelling. But everybody in the EBO should have at least two versions of the five most frequently used story types prepared:

– Geoffrey Moore's version. For (target customer) who (statement of the need) our (product/ service is a/an (product category) that (statement of benefit)
Example: "For windmill operators who want to maximize asset up-time, our product is a Predictive Maintenance service that eliminates unplanned downtime."

- Steve Blank's version. We help (customer) do (job-to-be-done) by providing (value proposition)
  Example: "We help people to buy and sell digital services in the same fashion as physical goods by providing an e-commerce platform."

- Clayton Christensen's version. We help to (verb) (object of action) (contextual identifier)
  Example: "We help to manage personal finances at home."

- Barbara Minto's version. (Situation: What is the current situation?) (Complication: the issue in the situation) (Question, related to the issue) (Answer: suggest a solution to ease out or mitigate the issue).
  Example: People who recover from an accident should continue the physical exercises that the therapist recommended at home. Yet 70% of patients do not do this. As a result, they recover much more slowly or not at all. How can we motivate patients to do physical therapy exercises at home? By gamification – a webcam feeds the patient's movements to a video game. This makes the exercises simple to understand and more entertaining.

- David Cowan's version. (Highlight the enormity of the problem) (Tell the audience up front what the startup sells) (Distill the differentiation down to one sentence) (establish credibility).
  Example: "One person dies of melanoma every 62 minutes. We offer an app that enables people to diagnose their skin, leveraging pattern recognition technology trusted by the WHO."

Chapter

09
FREQUENT MISTAKES
AND BEST PRACTICES

Six essential insights in this chapter.

You will find these again within the text.

 Interviews are an essential part of innovation work. However, only a few companies invest in training innovation interview skills. They leave it to the EBO's leader.

This bears substantial risks. The company also leaves insights that might help Core's marketing and sales on the table.

 Many problems in building new businesses from innovation arise at the very first milestone.

In too many cases, "reasons to believe" are confused with problem/solution-fit. The former explains why an innovation idea makes sense. They are a good starting point but not a solid foundation for a future business.

 MVPs are optimized for learning, not scaling. Often, this is hard to convey to engineers who have been building to build, not building to learn in their careers.

While the EBO team decides what "Minimum" means, the customer determines "Viable."

 Many EBOs think that they have achieved product/market-fit when they book the first customers. This is wrong.

With the first customers, the EBO has product/pioneer-fit, but not product/market-fit. Pioneer customers approach new tech differently than mainstream customers.

 Product/market fit marks the end goal of the learning phase. It is not a finish line that the EBO reaches on a particular day, but rather a spectrum that ranges from "very poor" to "very good."

I think it would be better to speak of the quality of the product/market-fit.

 Companies can use the Lean Scaleup's pre-Scaling process (see chapter 7) to upgrade their EBO portfolio management.

For this purpose, a portfolio diagram is helpful, which shows the stages of the innovation journey, how long a particular EBO has been in its respective stage, and the investments into the startup in the last 12 months.

CHAPTER 09

Frequent mistakes and Best Practices

*"Remember that you are looking for the best answer
not merely the best answer that you can come up with yourself."*

Ray Dalio

Chapter 7 described the Lean Scaleup methodology. This chapter is an add-on to that. It highlights Best Practices and ten mistakes that I frequently see in my client work. The mistakes shown are not intended to downplay the hard work of EBOs[61]. These people are already smart – this chapter is the chance to get even smarter by knowing the most significant potholes and where other companies excel.

Innovation interviews

One of the prerequisites for building a new business from innovation is deep customer understanding. This deep understanding requires meaningful innovation interviews with carefully selected potential customers.

Interviews are needed in the business foundation stage to uncover mission-critical problems that the company could solve better than anyone else. In my experience,

- an EBO that uses the corporate brand ("we are from company xyz and our company wants to …") should plan for at least 8 interviews,

---

61 "Emerging Business Opportunities" which stands for corporate startups/ventures

- a mid-market company for at least 20,

- and an EBO that is not using the corporate brand for more than 30.

Interviews are also essential in later stages, such as in the business strategy stage, to understand which features of a Minimum Viable Product (MVP) provide the most value in the customer's eyes.

 However, **only a few companies invest in raising the bar for interview skills**. They leave interviewing quality to the EBO's leader. They are to select the right interview partners, structure the interview and find the right tonality. In my view, this approach is not optimal:

- It bears the substantial risk that a new business's foundation and strategy are not reliable, putting a question mark on the overall success chances.

- It does not help the company to build excellence in the early stages of innovation.

- Since insights from innovation interviews help understand customers better, Core's Sales and Marketing do not benefit.

Good innovation interviews are not Q&A sessions with pre-fabricated questions. They are a conversation aiming at extracting and discovering valuable insights. They are not about asking the customer what they think about the solution – inevitably, this will influence the interview partner[62].

In the business foundation stage, I recommend not discussing the solution idea at all. The conversation should instead be about exploring the problem space surrounding the intended solution. In the business strategy stage, innovation interviews should explore the specific value points of the MVP. And in the business design phase, the goal should be to examine the quality of product/market-fit (see below).

---

62 There is a brilliant book on how to conduct innovation interviews: Rob Fitzpatrick, "The Mom Test"

Problem/solution-fit

Problem/solution-fit is one deliverable of the business foundation stage. It provides the initial proof that the basic idea could become a sizable, profitable business.

Many argue that innovation should start with the (customer) problem and not with the solution. Although this customer-centric argument is generally acceptable, I have a slightly different view. I have worked with many tech EBOs who had a solution – for example, a new Digital tool or a new material – and searched for the right problem (see below).

I think the issue is not so much if the problem or the solution comes first. The point is much more that there is **the first gateway – problem/solution-fit – that any new business needs to pass through**. The subsequent stages of the innovation journey would be the same, no matter if the innovation idea came from the customer side ("problem looking for a solution") or from the tech side ("solution looking for a problem"). It is the rigor in applying the methodology (see chapter 7) and the right mindset (see chapter 8) that count.

What problem/solution-fit is (not)

I have witnessed many situations in which "reasons to believe" were called problem/solution-fit. "Reasons to believe" explain why an innovation idea makes sense. Typically, these come from statistics in consultant reports, a gut feeling that "there is a market out there," strategy exercises, and ideation sessions about "what else could we do with our core competence?"

I also see that technical prototypes or lab samples are considered to have problem/solution-fit because "they offer benefits for the customer." I do not think that this is right. **It is not the innovator but the customer who defines the benefits** and if they would switch from an existing solution and well-established workarounds or not. Often, they do not want to change because it is risky, incurs costs, and requires process changes and learning efforts.

"Reasons to believe" are excellent starting points for the innovation journey, but they are not problem/solution-fit. **They lack validation in field research via interviews with actual persons, not just statistics.** Statistics will tell that the average machine has an unplanned downtime once per week, and the lab sample may have superior lubrication qualities. But only the field research will show that the machine is dirty and the real problem is maintenance.

The field research also needs to validate two more things before the EBO can be sure to have achieved problem/solution-fit:

- The **problem is high on the customers' priority list**. Only when the problem is important or urgent – ideally, it is mission-critical – customers will consider switching from the existing solution and pay for the new one

- The **innovation's timing fits with the customer's innovation cycle**. In some industries (e.g., Automotive), customers innovate in multi-year cycles; when the innovation launch misses the window of opportunity, it is not relevant for customers

Are you working on the right problem?

How should a future gas station be designed – with the knowledge that even with the increasing penetration of electric vehicles, petrol-powered cars will remain the dominant automobile for the following years? I have asked this question to hundreds of senior managers. They typically suggest things like including a coffee shop, making the station an Amazon drop-off point, or having robots pump gas. Their rationale for such changes is to provide additional value to customers.

But are these ideas addressing the job the customer is trying to do – conveniently refuel the car? Are they indeed customer-centric? No, they are not. Most people consider driving to the gas station an unavoidable inconvenience. If people need to refill their vehicles but dislike getting gas – how can one solve this problem? Not by putting Starbucks in gas stations. But what if we could bring the petrol to the cars? Several startups have already built a business on this idea.

Almost every company believes it is customer-centric. But I think that most are product-centric. They focus on enhancing their offerings (e.g., adding services to gas stations) rather than putting themselves in their customers' shoes (e.g., helping customers avoid the gas station altogether). Innovation is about solving customer problems that are high on the priority list and a willingness to pay for a solution. **It is not about products that, in the innovator's eye, should be important to customers.**

Most startups fail because they do not understand the problem correctly (see chapter 8). Yes, there are tools available that help the innovator to structure thinking. But I notice that many teams prefer clinging to tools than take the effort of hard thinking.

One example is the "customer journey map," which is a visual representation of the customer's journey and experiences across all touchpoints, before, during, and after buying a product. Nowadays, it is an essential tool for corporate innovators and leaders of EBOs. However, almost every customer journey map I see centers around the product.

Imagine a bank designing a mobile app for a mortgage. It might streamline steps in the application process to make it easier to search and apply for a mortgage. It might build algorithms to respond to their applications more rapidly and enable live chat with an agent to answer questions. This process is typical, but it is product-focused. It overlooks why the customer is seeking a mortgage.

One bank takes a different approach. The EBO thinks beyond products. The team realized that no one gets excited about buying a mortgage. The genuine excitement is in purchasing a future home. Concerning purchasing a mortgage, the customer journey begins long before customers consider applying for a mortgage.

So, the team investigated what helps customers find their dream house in the first place. They developed a mobile app that allows customers to scan a neighborhood's surroundings and view the latest transaction prices. When they find a home that appeals to them, a mortgage calculator helps them determine if they can afford it.

A product-centric approach bears the risk that the EBO works on the wrong problem. It is not the customer's job to know what their problems are. **Customers are often more solution-oriented than problem-oriented.**

They usually have difficulty articulating the problem they are trying to solve and identifying its root causes. The hard thinking work remains with the innovators – "innovators innovate and customers validate."

Love the problem, not the solution

The EBO needs to fall in love with the right problem, not the solution. Only when it profoundly understands the problem and all relevant aspects, it can develop a meaningful solution and a solid business foundation.

Unfortunately, too many EBOs rush to solutions before they have fully understood the problem. This is somewhat understandable. Checking the tickbox labeled "problem/solution-fit" conveys the feeling of progress. But of course, it is not real progress. It is only a step in the wrong direction.

It is easy to jump to solutions when the facts are weak. When the team does not engage in innovation interviews, there are only opinions. Hard facts come from observation and not from surveys because:

- Survey respondents may understand the question differently than intended.

- They may imagine a completely different solution or struggle to express their imagination in the answers provided.

- A survey response does not mean any commitment.

- Survey results do not tell the story – they will not disclose that the machine is dirty, covered in oil, and has not been maintained for a long time (see above).

Sometimes, I see problem statements that offer only one meaningful solution. I recommend that the EBOs rethink them. When faced with this situation, instead of jumping to a singular solution, the team should go back and review how they got here in the first place. The fishbone diagram, also known as the Ishikawa diagram, the "5 Whys" and pivots (see below) are helpful tools in such a situation.

I believe that **in many cases, a team's tendency to love the solution more than the problem traces back to their company's climate:**

- There is a company culture that puts brilliant presentations above evidence-based research.

- Senior managers push to find quick fixes and the realization of short-term goals.

- Management falls in love with a solution too quickly because it provides the good but a false-positive feeling of progress.

Ideal problems

Finding a real customer problem that is "worth to be solved" is the foundation of a potential sizable and sustainable new business. As described in chapter 7, many validations are necessary to make a final call if a meaningful idea could indeed become a sizable and profitable business.

A quick litmus test shows the team early if the identified problem could justify this validation work. This litmus test qualifies problems:

- **Size.** Exciting problems are widespread: many customers have the problem.

- **Large market inefficiencies.** Removing inefficiencies in large, existing markets (such as Amazon did for retail, Airbnb for hospitality, and Uber for transportation) spares the EBO to create a market.

- **Growth.** Good problems are growing: more and more customers will have the problem in the future.

- **Frequent.** Good problems tend to be encountered by customers often, over a specific and measured time interval.

- **Urgent.** Good problems need to be solved as soon as possible.

- **Cost-efficient.** Good problems have an interesting payback period for the customers.

- **High willingness to pay.** It does not make sense to start the innovation journey when customers do not refinance the costs via purchasing the problem solution.

- **Mandatory.** Good problems are somehow enforced, e.g., by regulation, legal contracts, or technological shifts.

How to tell that you have achieved problem/solution-fit

Even when the team found a good problem (see above) and validated it via field research, it is sometimes hard to decide if the EBO has achieved the problem/solution-fit. I witnessed some situations when there were too many unknowns in the context of the problem. When the EBO discussed whether it should invest more time exploring the problem or moving on, I recommend using the "skin in the game" test.

"Skin in the game" is a metaphor for some activity with a possibility of winning or losing something of value in that game (e.g., money, time, or reputation). **Before an EBO puts a lot of "skin in the game," it should make sure that it can get some from the target market.** The test is whether some potential customers show some level of commitment. Since this is very early in the innovation journey, the commitment will be limited. One meaningful commitment would be to spend time discussing the functionality of future prototypes or an MVP. Even better would be a commitment to co-develop the product after the MVP.

If none of the interviewed customers do this, then the team can't count those people as likely customers. They are merely spectators – they have got nothing to lose. They might even enjoy watching the team and the idea crash and burn.

Getting the technical pilot right

Early-stage EBOs need to demonstrate their product's technical capabilities via a technical pilot – sometimes, this is also called a "proof-of-concept." However, most of these initiatives die after such a pilot. For example, companies scale only 10-13 percent of EBOs that build their value proposition on Artificial Intelligence or Internet-Of-Things beyond this point[63].

Of course, there might be purely technical reasons to stop the work – for instance, when the technical pilot's performance was not convincing. But I also hear corporate stakeholders speaking about cases when the technical

---

63 https://www.capgemini.com/wp-content/uploads/2020/09/Scaling-Innovation_Infographic-3.pdf

performance was promising, but the EBO did not advance beyond this point. There is so much potential left on the table.

So how should companies change their approach to technical pilots to increase the percentage of EBOs that make it beyond the technical pilot stage (assuming that the technical performance is promising)? The more than 20 companies that co-created the Lean Scaleup found **six strategies to increase the likelihood of success**.

- **Senior Management's skin in the game.** A carefully selected technical pilot is more than just a technical pastime. It holds the promise of a step-change in the business process's technological performance, commercial benefits, or maybe even a cornerstone for a new business. For all these reasons, Senior Management should be engaging.

- **Align with KPI improvements.** The technical pilot's goals need to be expressed in the KPIs that matter for the operative business to win Senior Management's attention. The technical pilot must be designed to deliver a precise measure around a defined business outcome.

- **Avoid the "pilot trap."** Once Senior Management is engaged and the technical pilot's goals expressed in business KPIs, the EBO and corporate stakeholders should – even before the technical pilot starts – agree on the next step after a successful pilot and sketch out a pathway to scale up this technology.

- **Make everyone look good.** Too often, there is an "us and them" in technical pilots. There are often smart "Digital natives" on the one side and thoughtful, seasoned, experienced engineers who lack Digital skills but know and care about their processes on the other side. In my view, a successful technical pilot is always a joint effort between the "old world" and the "new world."

- **De-risk it.** The EBO should aim to make the technical pilot "Hippocratic," i.e., do not produce harm. Operational data must be protected, and there should be minimal interference with ongoing systems and processes. Technical pilots must be quick and easy to shut down, and they must not create novel vulnerability.

- **Less is more.** Often, the EBO tries to pack many tests into one. I challenge the team to focus on the one most critical insight to acquire. They should not focus on the top two or the top three – only on the most important one. This helps align with engineers and Senior Management; it reduces setup time and typically increases the quality of learnings from the technical pilot.

Minimum Viable Product

As Eric Ries wrote[64], a Minimum Viable Product (MVP) is a learning tool. Any additional work beyond what was needed to learn is a waste, no matter how important it might have seemed at the time.

The term MVP has become mainstream in innovation. In my view, a better word would have been "**Minimum Valuable Product**" – a precursor to the product with customer value in the spotlight, but a minimum set of features. But since the term Minimum Viable Product has become mainstream innovation language, the Lean Scaleup framework uses this term as well.

MVPs are optimized for learning, not scaling. **Often, this is hard to convey to engineers who have been building to build, not building to learn in their careers.** Some of the EBO clients that I work with also find it hard to grasp that **while the EBO team decides what "Minimum" means (see below), the customer determines "Viable."**

Never have I experienced a team that had a smashing success with the first MVP. It takes a team weeks or even months of build-test-measure-learn until they hit the bull's eye.

Example of a real MVP

There is an illuminating story about what a real MVP is and how to use it in the innovation journey. The company is Square, a Financial Services company with more than USD 100bn market capitalization. Square's initial

---

64 Eric Ries, "The Lean Startup"

vision was to build a commerce ecosystem that helps sellers start, run, and grow their business. The products turn mobile and desktop computing devices into payment and point-of-sale solutions. Square then saw the opportunity to build a similar ecosystem of services for individuals, providing financial access to all and allowing anyone to send, spend, and save money all from one app.

At that time, the only way to connect a credit card scanner to an iPhone was by using Apple's proprietary 30-pin dock connector. Apple had a lengthy approval process, required defined chipsets, asked for royalties for every unit sold, and requested compliance with Apple-defined rules. Square's EBO noticed that iPhones – like other smartphones at that time – had a microphone jack. So, if the team could turn credit card data into sound signals, any iPhone could acquire and process this data. Since Apple's audio software kit was publicly available, the team could write the software and have a working prototype within one week without asking anyone at Apple for permission.

What an MVP is (not)

I have seen many cases in which MVPs are built with significant engineering efforts. They almost resemble the final product – for instance, they have neatly designed user interfaces and carefully crafted reporting functionalities. The risk is that the efforts that went into developing such a sophisticated prototype might be more or less wasted when core functionalities that solve the customer problem are underdeveloped.

An MVP is not a work of art. It is a tool to validate hypotheses and discover which features have the highest priority from the customer's view. Each version of the MVP serves this purpose. When it has fulfilled its mission, the EBO replaces it with something better. MVPs are used in a fully-controlled environment, such as pre-arranged demonstration meetings – they are not supposed to be used by customers in their environment (which is one of the significant differences between an MVP and a Minimum Marketable Product).

I see too many EBOs that spend time perfecting something that they call MVP instead of developing rapid iterations and discussing them with potential customers. The reason might be that some people find it easier to do some engineering work in the office than to get outside and potentially receive "unpleasant feedback."

I think there are **two psychological traps in over-engineering an MVP**:

- The more time a team invests in something, the more valuable it becomes for the team – though not necessarily for the customer!

- Customers might be hesitant to provide honest feedback in innovation interviews. They want to be friendly to the EBO and do not want to hurt the feelings of the people who have put so much work into a product that "looks quite good."

These psychological traps might lead to poor decision-making. Spending too much time on individual prototypes reduces the time the team can spend on learning. Consequently, I recommend my clients to **timebox MVP iteration loops.** When there are time constraints, the team needs to prioritize and focus relentlessly, to look at the "core of the core" only.

What should be in an MVP?

Many EBOs focus more on an MVP's features than on the customer problem and customer value. To get an MVP right, they should focus on the why before the what and define customer value before product features.

When I coach EBOs at the business strategy stage – i.e., with the product at the MVP maturity stage – I challenge them to **assume that the customer does not care about the product**: they do not have the time to use it, do not ponder switching from the existing solution, skip any onboarding tutorials, do not read what is on the screen, and forget about it after the demo.

From this hypothesis, we **then develop something that rings a bell for potential customers.** So an MVP should not be something ugly, glued and soldered together that shows some functionality. In my work, I typically use a four-step ladder to organize the thinking:

- Functionality (core and housekeeping)

- Reliability

- Usability

- Delight

We then cut across these four levels and identify the elements that should go into the next iteration. Working under a self-imposed time constraint, the team always asks, "what can we build rapidly and cheaply?"

On the functional level, I find it helpful to distinguish between core and housekeeping functionality. The former defines a few singular value points that should be validated in upcoming customer interviews. The latter comprises a bare minimum set of features of what a modern user would expect from any comparable product.

Minimum Marketable Product and product/pioneer-fit

After the product has reached the MVP maturity level, the EBO collaborates with potential customers to develop a first version of the product for use in their environment. The environment is the big, qualitative jump between an MVP and a Minimum Marketable Product (MMP): the former is in an environment under complete control of the EBO (e.g., pre-arranged demonstration meetings), while the latter is in the customer environment.

These co-developing potential customers are almost always visionary and open to innovation. They:

- appreciate discussing new, not yet perfect, but ahead-of-the-curve concepts,

- are innovation/technology leaders in their industry (although they may not be the biggest company),

- pursue the first-to-market strategy,

- are actively looking for a competitive edge by using next-generation technology,

- have the ability to find new uses for a technology,

- and are prepared to use a product that is not yet complete.

The "Crossing the Chasm" framework[65] calls these customers pioneers (some call them "innovators" or "tech enthusiasts"). Pioneers and early

---

65 Geoffrey Moore, "Crossing the Chasm"

adopters buy first, and then – with a chasm in-between – mainstream customers, which represent the most significant part of the market.

Mainstream customers' approach to new technology is fundamentally different from pioneers' and early adopters' approaches. They ask for references and success stories because they expect a high probability of implementation success before engaging in in-depth discussions. When they finally engage, they expect a "full product" – a complete solution that includes the product, full-blown certification, integrations of the product with their existing infrastructure, and meaningful services.

There are hundreds of case studies showing that the marketing and sales chasm between pioneers/early adopters and mainstream customers is genuine and not just theory. One example that I have witnessed is a corporate venture trying to bring new cost-efficiency to an industry with a machine-learning software suite.

After booking the first customers, the corporate venture assumed that it had reached product/market-fit. Anticipating a surge in customers and revenues, it recruited a sizable sales team. However, it did not make significant progress. Key metrics, such as the number of potential clients in the sales funnel, the average revenue per customer, or the sales cycle's length, did not improve.

I suggested taking a step back and take a fresh look at market segments. We identified mainstream customers from participant lists of recent industry conferences and arranged innovation interviews. It turned out that the "full product" that these customers expected was less about the technological sophistication of the machine-learning algorithms. Their needs were getting clear decision support from the software, practical help in identifying relevant sensor data, arranging meaningful trials, receive support in adopting and rolling out the technology, and getting help in technical integration with adjacent IT solutions.

Product/pioneer-fit, not product/market-fit

I often see that EBOs are not thoughtful enough regarding how to work with pioneer customers. On the one hand, having a pioneer customer is excellent news. The team gets the chance to develop an MMP with a real-life customer and ensure that product features align with customer expectations. Additionally, the EBO has its first reference customers, which is essential for winning mainstream customers.

But on the other hand, **pioneer customers' problems might be years ahead of mainstream customers' problems.** And these problems might be so sophisticated that they never become an issue for mainstream customers. **In this case, the EBO would build a solution that only applies to a tiny fraction of the market.**

Assuming that pioneer and early adopter customers are representative for the whole market and starting Scaling-Up is wrong (see the example above). Scaling-Up after the first customer is one of the most frequent mistakes that EBOs make. It leads almost inevitably to premature Scaling-Up (see chapter 7).

When a pioneer customer puts his "skin in the game," **the EBO has achieved product/pioneer-fit, but not product/market-fit**.

The Lean Scaleup methodology urges EBOs to explore the mainstream customer segment when the product is at the MMP maturity level – i.e., at the business design stage – to avoid this mistake. The EBO needs to validate that the value proposition appeals to mainstream customers and that it can win them within a reasonable time and with adequate customer acquisition cost.

Product/market-fit

Paraphrasing tech innovator and Silicon Valley VC Marc Andreessen, the life of a successful EBO can be divided into two phases: before product/market-fit and Scaling-Up after product/market-fit. All previous steps, such as problem/solution-fit and MVP, are only prologue; they provide increasing certainty that the EBO is on the right way and that further funding to move to the next stage is justified.

The threshold that counts is **the proof that the EBO is in a good market with a product that can satisfy that market** – this is product/market-fit. When the goal is to disrupt an industry or create a new category, **being the first to market is not what counts. Being first to product/market-fit makes the difference** (see the examples in chapter 2).

Product/market-fit is one of the essential prerequisites for the Scaling-Up decision. But many EBOs are not at product/market-fit when they think they are. In some instances, a wrong understanding of product/market-fit (see the example above) offers an explanation. In other cases, teams do not think far enough:

- The real focus needs to be the value proposition, not the product itself. No company is in the business of producing and selling a product. All companies are in the business of solving customer problems – for which a product is an intermediary. Consequently, **the EBO competes against all companies that offer a solution for the customer to get the job done** – not only companies that make a comparable product.

- The market definition might be too narrow and hence does not cover the solutions that customers evaluate "to get the job done." Markets and whole industries continuously change: the Automotive market is becoming a mobility market, and companies are switching from buying production equipment to using production equipment as a service. **Markets are never static and never defined by the product.**

A quality indicator, not a finish line

 Product/market fit marks the end of the learning phase. It is not a finish line that the EBO reaches on a particular day but rather a spectrum that ranges from "very poor" to "very good." I think **it would be better to speak of the quality of the product/market-fit.**

This quality depends on two forces that pull mainstream customers towards or away from buying the innovation – the restraining force and the driving force. Customer concerns increase the restraining force, and a successfully validated product capability reduces it. If the balance of forces changes in favor of the driving force, the product/market-fit's quality improves.

EBOs typically underestimate the restraining force. Often, it has little to no relation to the actual functionality of the product. For example, in large corporates, politics or bureaucracy may prevent a decision to buy, independent of how substantial the technical buyer's benefits are.

The restraining force more often comes from a small number of significant concerns than from the sum of many smaller factors. For example, an enterprise customer expects to have guaranteed availability of machine replacement parts over the whole usage time; if the supplier cannot guarantee this, a purchase is out of the question.

Frequently, EBOs encounter these concerns:

- The costs for switching from the existing solution to the innovation are too high.

- Switching creates a new problem.

- To use the product, the customer must do something they do not want to do.

- The product causes an internal conflict.

- The purchase of the product contradicts an internal rule.

- The product introduces a new risk.

- The product does not fit with the existing infrastructure.

- The customer has an opinion that speaks against the product.

- The customer lacks the knowledge required to use the product.

- The potential benefits of the product are not apparent (or not credible) to the customer.

- The use of the product is cumbersome.

Traction metrics

It is not always apparent whether the quality of a product/market-fit is good enough, and there is no formula to calculate it. So the EBO needs to **find empirical indicators to judge the quality of the product/market-fit.** These indicators are called "traction metrics." They are leading indicators for future revenues.

Traction metrics that my clients use include:

- Success rate in customer acquisition (which should be continuously improving)

- Costs of acquiring a new customer (decreasing and lower than the lifetime value of a new customer)

- Speed of customer's purchase decision (increasing)

- Customers' views on the superiority of value proposition (an increasing part of new customers state that the innovation is far superior to other offerings that they have considered or even tested)

- Churn rate, measuring customer loyalty (decreasing)

- Product usage, measuring the proportion of new customers who use the product intensively (increasing)

- Net Promoter Score, i.e., the proportion of customers who recommend the product to others (growing)

- Sean Ellis test (when trial users are asked, "how would you feel if you could no longer use the product?" an increasing number of respondents answer "very disappointed")

Traction is the most crucial evidence for corporate investors to convince themselves that the EBO is "worthy to be scaled." Conversely, if EBOs start Scaling-Up without significant traction – and hence, without a high-quality product/market-fit – they are likely to fail due to premature Scaling (see chapter 7).

But what if the EBO cannot provide enough proof of traction? I once was asked by the CEO of a corporate venture, "what if we don't find enough trial users from the mainstream customer segment to demonstrate traction?" I replied, "then you probably haven't even found problem/solution-fit."

The art of pivoting

Building a new business from innovation bears a lot of uncertainty. Initially, an EBO has many ideas about potential customers, why they will buy, the suitable business model, and the revenues and profits that such a business could create, etc. But these are all assumptions. And typically, the list of assumptions is not complete when the team starts the innovation journey.

At some point, the EBO might find that some fundamental assumptions do not withstand the reality check. When there is enough reason to believe in the original idea, it is time to adapt and change the course. This is called "pivoting."

When they keep their shareholders aligned, VC-backed greenfield start-ups may pivot along their entire journey until they find a scalable business model that creates significant revenues and profits. There are famous examples of great companies that pivoted to success. Twitter launched as a platform for subscribing to podcasts, YouTube started as a dating site, and PayPal was initially a security software company.

EBOs have a lesser degree of freedom to pivot since they are not only a financial play. Their additional mission is delivering a piece of the strategic corporate innovation and transformation agenda. Hence EBOs should only pivot in the first three stages of the innovation journey – the business foundation, business strategy, or the business design stage. A pivot in Scaling-Up might be too difficult to arrange in the corporate context.

Pivots in the business foundation stage are pretty standard. By definition, the corporate startup is searching for a sustainable and scalable business model. Pivoting at this stage does not mean an uncoordinated trial-and-error, however. Effective pivoting builds on careful evaluation of the preceding learning loops and makes well-thought-through adjustments. Pivoting is not a buzzword-excuse to skip the hard thinking.

I find it helpful to go through the potential pivots in a pre-arranged ladder and explore each step on the ladder before hopping to the next. The steps of the ladder are:

- **Solution pivot.** Should we target another solution or a different business model to solve the identified customer problem?

- **Problem pivot.** Are we targeting the right problem?

- **Jury pilot.** Are we talking to the right people to get the validation we need?

- **Market pivot.** Are we targeting the right market, in which a problem sits that we can solve better than anyone else?

- **Vision pivot.** Should we change the basic idea?

The market pivot relates to the question "where should we play?". Due to the corporate context in which the EBO operates, this option requires realignment with the corporate stakeholders. The vision pivot is the last option because it means starting over. It can be highly disappointing for the stakeholders and the startup team.

There are differentiated options for **pivots in the business strategy and the business design stages**. At this stage, there is a clearer view of future product features and the underlying business model. I use a pivoting framework that builds on the elements of the Business Model Canvas:

- **Zoom pivots.** A feature of the product is so valuable that it becomes the whole product. Or, conversely, the initial innovation is included in an even more extensive product or platform.

- **Value proposition pivot.** When pioneers and early adopters (in the business strategy stage) or mainstream customers (in the business design stage) do not see the value, changing the value proposition might be an option. For instance, switching from a product-centered to a services-centered business model (or vice versa) might be pivoting options.

- **Value creation pivot.** Changing the dependency on suppliers by reintegration or offloading key activities to suppliers are options.

- **Value delivery pivot.** When the solution had value in the customers' eyes, a new go-to-market strategy or a new revenue model might be an option.

- **Customer pivots.** When the initially targeted customers do not see the problem to be significant, pivoting to another customer segment is an option.

A layout for financial projections

Since EBOs target new-to-the-company ambitions, it is quite a stretch for many corporate stakeholders to think through the financial projections and implications that the EBOs present to them. The challenge increases when the company has many EBOs in different stages.

To ensure better alignment between EBOs and corporate stakeholders, some of my clients have decided to use a standardized layout for financial projections. They find a structure with four sections – income statement, cash flow and valuation, balance sheet, and non-financial KPIs – helpful.

The **income statement section** contains in 1/3/5-year time horizons:
- Major financial assumptions, such as market size, pricing model, customer growth, customer acquisition costs, and customer lifetime value
- Revenues
- COGS (cost of goods sold)
- Other operating expenditures
- Per-unit gross margin (e.g., per customer or contract)
- EBITDA (earnings before interest, taxes, depreciation, and amortization)

The **cash flow and valuation section** contains in 1/3/5-year time horizons free cash flow, burn rate (and financial runway, if relevant), valuation, and future funding requirements.

The **balance sheet section** shows in 1/3/5-year time horizons capital expenditures/assets and liabilities – which are particularly important for asset-heavy innovations. Finally, the **non-financial KPIs section** contains metrics related to financial projections (such as traction metrics) or the corporate context (such as cannibalization of the existing core business).

With increasing maturity, the dimensions mentioned above are populated and detailed. For instance, at the end of the business foundation stage, when there is a high degree of uncertainty, the financial projection layout comprises:

- Major financial assumptions – Indicative market size, shortlist of Serviceable Available Markets (SAMs) with indicative sizes, the indicative total number of customers in the entire market and the SAMs (all with a 3-year perspective), validated pricing models and willingness-to-pay

- Revenues - Indicative revenue size in 3 years

- Other operating expenditures – Assumptions about personnel costs ("would this be a people-intensive business?")

- Valuation – Initial valuation based on market capitalization multiples of comparable companies

- Funding - Funds needed to get to the end of the business strategy and the business design stages (i.e., MVP and MMP product maturity)

- Size and type of significant capital expenditures ("would this be an asset-heavy business?")

Working with corporate ventures

In theory, there are compelling reasons for corporate/startup relationships. The company gets access to the startup's creativity, agile ways of working, and new technologies. In contrast, the startup gets access to pioneer customers, the company's markets, industry expertise, and a firm reference.

The practice, however, is sobering. Companies' ten most essential expectations are fulfilled only to 50 percent – and startups see five out of their ten crucial expectations fulfilled by only 20-35 percent. Interestingly, companies' and startups' views on why these relationships fail are relatively homogeneous, with three notable exceptions. Companies do not see mutual recognition and cooperation on equal footing; startups see a lack of steering and governance and the companies' inability to deal with different mindsets and cultures[66].

---

66 https://www.bcg.com/de-de/publications/2019/corporate-startup-relationships-work-after-honey-moon-ends

How external ventures see the business-building problem

In my work, I discussed with many corporate ventures the decisive factors for success in Scaling-Up. Looking at it from a different angle, the insights from these conversations also helped deepen my understanding of the corporate business-building problem.

Typical corporate ventures do not have a clear view of the business-building problem of their corporate investors. But excellent ones do. The former fall into the traps of corporate/startup relationships, whereas the latter navigate the company's shortcomings – especially a disconnect between innovation and Core.

When I discussed the challenges for corporates to create new businesses, some of the corporate ventures were very outspoken. One CEO said, "it seems like we are a show pony;" another one said, "we are here for entertainment purposes," and a third one complained that "we are just a line item in the corporate innovation funnel." It seems that, ironically, the issue is more prominent when the corporate venture has a product, not just technology. When there is a product, all corporate stakeholders have opinions – but only a few experts cast their voices when there is just technology.

Excellent external ventures see the **downsides and the risks of engaging with disconnected innovation units.** If it is not watchful, the venture is locked in a place with little power to change the status quo. Consequently, its chances to engage with Core's functions – particularly Core's sales force – are limited.

Excellent ventures understand that they need to talk to the right people from Core and show how they could help in improving business KPIs. They know that stakeholder management is as essential as getting the technical pilot right. They **start a technical pilot only when there is a game plan for what would happen after the end of the pilot** – such as an agreement on the next steps. Excellent ventures recognize the warning signals when a technical pilot is likely not to lead anywhere and stay away from these situations.

Eight success factors

The companies who co-created the Lean Scaleup framework distilled their Best Practices for working with corporate ventures into eight success factors.

Companies need to **be clear on why they are working with corporate ventures**. There are four primary motivations. Depending on the company's preference, they influence how collaboration should play out:

- Build new business models, products, or services that support and protect the core business

- Optimize functions, such as R&D, operations, and marketing/sales

- Grow into adjacent areas

- Use a startup's outsider mindset and new skills to transform and move away from its core business.

An **effective collaboration model** should be the foundation for collaboration. I advise my clients to set up one page (not twenty!) which outlines – specifically for each side – the expected value from the collaboration, the rewards, the specific contributions, and the risks.

A lean collaboration governance should define responsibilities and decision rights, concerning, for example, which party decides what, in which situations can each partner act independently, and when do the parties need to coordinate and align on decisions.

The company should also **arrange access to corporate assets** for the startup to increase the collaboration's value, if relevant. Generally, all corporate assets mentioned in chapter 2 are worth considering.

In many cases, the company assigns only one manager who overlooks the corporate/startup relationship. This practice creates a bottleneck for the startup. It is also challenging for this manager as well – they need to run internal promotion campaigns to link the corporate venture with Core's functions. **Instilling the right mindset on a broad base** helps the internal champion. It also broadens the base of Core managers who drive transformation.

As stated above, many corporate/startup relationships fail because there is an "us and them" mentality and little mutual respect. The company and the startup should **embrace the differences**. They should also **communicate as equal partners**. This includes avoiding power games, creating a shared vision of the future together, articulating it, and regularly making time to discuss the progress.

Finally, companies need to **accept failure**. Most startups will not succeed. Companies need to pull the plug when conditions warrant their doing so – and if the relationship is not working out, the earlier, the better.

Integration of tech startups

Most large companies do not have corporate venture capital (CVC) units. Depending on the definition, there are only 139 to 179 of them in the US and Europe[67]. In the last years, some of the world's most innovative companies have found a clever way to actively engage external startups without the cost and risk associated with CVC.

These companies apply **an approach that combines intelligent and small investments with innovation management and suitable procurement processes.** In this approach, the company integrates outstanding startups into innovation projects as formal suppliers. To qualify, the startups need to be outstanding concerning technology and management – the latter measured by significant VC investment, graduation by a renowned accelerator, or a serial entrepreneur in the startup's leadership team.

In this approach, the three main parties – startups, private VCs and the company – focus on what they do best. Startups put their innovative technology to use in real-life projects and gain a reference and valuable insight into a corporate's workings, which helps them become savvier at business development. Being the flagship client for startups helps the company attract top startups and get first access to cutting-edge technology, time-to-market, and the chance to influence product design. VCs and accelerators increase their deal flow and apply their proven frameworks to sort out high-potential startups from the also-rans and to nurture them through their nascence.

---

67 https://www.sciencedirect.com/science/article/pii/S1544612318302411

The approach is not a corporate accelerator that typically offers guided programs with workshops and coaching, co-working space, corporate contacts, and an investment of up to USD 100k in return for equity. It is also not a technical proof-of-concept that aims to validate the performance of the startup's technology.

In essence, the company buys the corporate venture's technology for real pilot projects within the company's operative business units. The startup becomes an actual supplier, with purchase orders and supplier numbers, from day one. The initial purchase order is typically in the range of USD 10k, but both the company and the startup aim for a long-term, strategic partnership.

Throughout the pilot project and the multi-month collaboration, the company quickly becomes the startup's lead customer and has the opportunity to influence the product. When this influence is sustainably positive for the start-up, trust is also built up with the founding team and thus they prefer the company in financing rounds or purchase offers.

This approach needs, besides C-level sponsorship, four essential pieces:

- Agreement with corporate procurement that allows for issuing supplier numbers and purchase orders without a tender

- Cross-departmental budget for initial pilot projects – operative units will not be in a position to foresee this kind of pilot projects in their annual budgeting plan

- Intensive networking with VCs and accelerators to get early contact with promising startups

- Social marketing and PR to attract promising additional startups

Portfolio management with the Lean Scaleup

The probability of failure in building new businesses outside the core business is staggeringly high. There is no point in denying this reality. The consequence should be to use a robust process – which ranges from idea to scale – as the basis for identifying "walking dead" and pulling the plug on them early.

By doing so, the corporate firing power is behind those EBOs that are "worthy to be scaled" and "ready to be scaled." They have a higher chance to create business impact – and to achieve this goal more rapidly.

 Some of my clients have upgraded their EBO portfolio management with the Lean Scaleup methodology (see chapter 7) as the backbone of the process. For this purpose, a portfolio diagram is helpful. On the x-axis of this portfolio are the stages of the innovation journey. The y-axis measures how long a particular EBO has been in its respective stage. The bubble size represents the investments into the startup or innovation initiative in the last 12 months:

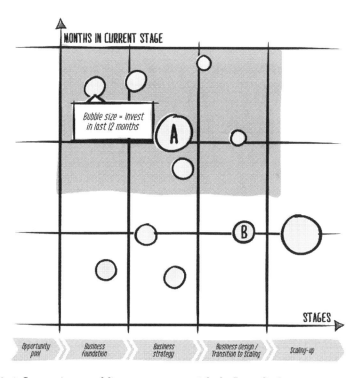

Figure 9-1: Improving portfolio management with the Lean Scaleup

This diagram identifies well-funded but slow-moving EBOs that could be prime candidates for pruning and redirecting their resources. In this example, one would look very critically at initiative A – this moves very slowly despite significant investments. The chart suggests that the company discusses whether it is more promising to divert money and human resources from this initiative into a fast-moving initiative such as B.

Chapter

10
SCALING-UP:
MARKET AND PRODUCT

Six essential insights in this chapter.

You will find these again within the text.

 Scaleups that succeed in making their market(s) are data-driven. They see customers as human beings and not just as functional objects called users.

They pay careful attention to the data trail their customers leave. Data is not only numbers; data is the customer's voice. The scaleup can learn from the data and improve in scalability.

 Selling an innovation through the well-oiled, highly efficient sales machine does not work in most cases.

In most companies, the scaleup cannot align with Core's sales force unless the system is adjusted. Adjusting the system is not a methodology issue – it requires dual leadership and adjusting the culture/collaboration (see chapter 5).

 During Scaling-Up, a scalable sales process needs to be developed to power rapid growth, drive down customer acquisition costs, onboard new staff, and learn at pace.

There also needs to be a scalable commercial apparatus that powers and enables this sales process.

 There are four types of product work: feature work, growth work, product/market-fit expansion work, and scaling work.

Not treating these separately leads to suboptimal processes, wrong success measures, and a weak alignment.

 Many scaleups think that adding new features is the natural thing to do in Scaling-Up.

There are many points in this view. But every new feature creates follow-on costs, "feature shadow costs."

There are three types of shadow costs.

 Customer experience is more important than product features. CTOs should spend time on customer support to get first-hand information about what customers like or dislike and what is missing.

Customers prefer excellent support and an above-average product to a great product and modest support.

CHAPTER 10

Scaling-Up: Market and product

*"Scaling a business at speed
can feel like an out-of-control roller-coaster."*

Taavet Hinrikus

Scaling a fast-growing corporate startup/venture always has its challenges. Fierce competition, countless options and traps, unexpected crises, funding concerns, managing stakeholder expectations and dreams, new technology developments, changing rules of ecosystems, operational challenges, changing laws, and much more can make a scaleup lose track quickly, plateau, get messy or decline.

Scaling-Up is the transition from a fully validated innovation concept that has been set up for success (see chapters 3, 7 and 9) to a sizable, profitable business that runs on the Efficiency/Predictability Paradigm of an established company (see chapter 3). From this point, it can further grow with proven methods such as product and process management, account and business development, and sophisticated financial controlling.

All transitions in innovation management are challenging – from foresight to strategy, from strategy to defining meaningful ideas, from meaningful ideas to validation, and from validation to scale. But Scaling-Up is the most challenging one for two reasons. Firstly, in Scaling-Up, the inherent conflict between the performance-oriented, risk-averse "Efficiency/Predictability Paradigm" of Core and the "Agility Paradigm" of innovation (see chapters 2 and 3) becomes apparent. Secondly, since the scaleup needs to do so many things, in so many areas, in such a short time, when it builds a sizable, profitable business in a few years, it is easy to lose control.

Succeeding in Scaling-Up needs good navigation instruments. The Lean Scaleup framework provides a guide for navigating the decisive aspects:

- Making the market

- Industrializing the product

- Growing the organization

- Establishing a culture of growth

This chapter looks into the first two of these aspects. The following chapter provides insight into the remaining two.

Making the market

 Success in winning new markets begins with the right mindset. Excellent scaleups see customers as human beings and not just as functional objects called users. With this mindset, they pay careful attention to the data trail their customers leave. **Data is not only numbers; data is the customer's voice.**

Any piece of data is a record of an action or event, which in most cases reflects a decision made by a human being. Hence, data is an indirect way of the customers telling what they like and do not like. If the scaleup can recreate the sequence of events leading up to that decision from the data trail, it can learn from it and improve scalability.

Measurement and data are essential elements of the scaleup's growth culture (see below). They help in mastering the market- and sales-related issues that I see frequently when working with scaleups.

Chasms, beachheads, and bowling alleys

When it comes to market success, assuming that a scaleup was "worthy of being scaled" and "ready to be scaled," what is the difference between successful scaleups and unsuccessful ones? I discussed this question with the more than 20 companies that co-created the Lean Scaleup framework. Since success leaves clues, we wanted to distill the essence for a scaleup's market success.

We think that there is a pattern. All scaleups that we analyzed segmented their Serviceable Available Markets and defined a priority market. This factor is not a differentiator. **The big difference seems to be what comes after the primary market.** Less successful scaleups did not say no to new customers from non-validated markets and got distracted. Successful scaleups executed the validated growth strategy that they developed pre-Scaling (see chapter 7).

One group of the successful scaleups that we analyzed was able to **"cross the chasm" and reach mainstream customers** in the large market with a superior, comprehensive solution. Mainstream customers expect a mature, "full product" comprising technical integrations and services that support implementation, onboarding, and roll-out (see chapters 7 and 9). Successful scaleups in this group excelled in making a move to an adequate go-to-market approach – engaging, for instance, Value Added Resellers or building affiliate programs. In this group, the market and tech teams work together well, and **the tech team does remarkable things in feature work and growth work** (see below).

We also found a second group of successful scaleups. They made their market by building a sequence of market successes. Scaleups from this group had a well-defined and validated growth strategy (see chapter 7) with a clear view of which markets to win after the first one. In their growth strategy, each subsequent market leveraged the previous one's technology and customers. Because these markets were related, reference customers from one market were familiar – and thus credible – to customers from the next one.

The successful scaleups from this group executed their growth strategy ruthlessly and said no to markets outside the validated scope. We also found that in this group's scaleups, tech and market teams collaborate very well, but differently: **tech teams excel in product/market-fit expansion work** (see below).

Geoffrey Moore[68] coined the phrase **"beachhead and bowling alley"** for the second group. The beachhead is the initial market, and the bowling

---

68 Geoffrey Moore, "Inside the tornado"

alley the markets that come next. Ideally, later-stage markets fall like the bowling pins after a carefully crafted throw. The Apple Macintosh computer is an excellent example of the "bowling alley." Apple sold it first to in-house graphics departments as a desktop publishing solution, then to marketing executives for business presentations, and then later into the professional prepress and publishing market.

Working together with Core's sales units

When there is a solid collaboration model in place, a scaleup can leverage corporate assets for an unfair advantage in the market and accelerate the journey (see chapter 5). Two important corporate assets are the operative business units' sales force and access to its customer base.

Core's salespeople know their customers and have earned their respect and trust. They understand how they need to influence the customer journey so that customers buy. So, in theory, there is a tremendous tailwind for the scaleup. However, in practice, it is hard for scaleups to align with Core's sales units. The deeper reason is that **these salespeople work in Core's performance-oriented, risk-averse "Efficiency/Predictability Paradigm,"** whereas the scaleup works under the incompatible "Agility Paradigm" (see chapter 2).

Professional salespeople are among the most rational people that I have met in my career. They are conscious about time because, to them, time is money. They are clear on where they should spend the last working hour of the week to close one more deal. They are also very efficient: they know their products, the sales story, how to engage the buying center, how to handle objections, and how to move the potential client through the sales funnel. They focus ruthlessly on short-term goals – the monthly or quarterly numbers. Additionally, they define their value partly by being an expert, trusted advisor, and "single point of contact" in their customers' eyes.

The innovation, i.e., **the product that the scaleup would like to sell through the sales force, does not fit at all into this efficient, well-oiled, and fast-turning sales machine**:

- Often, the innovation requires extensive explanation.

- Typically, the product builds on technologies (Artificial Intelligence, Internet-Of-Things, Blockchain, etc.) that the salespeople are not familiar with.

- When selling these products, the salespeople meet an unfamiliar buying center (including, for instance, the customer's Chief Digital Officer).

- And finally, the salesperson might not have the expertise to answer all questions and handle all objections, which challenges their expert image.

I have seen two approaches that work in aligning the sales units of the scaleup and Core. The first one plays out at the operational level. It builds on active and intensive collaboration of the scaleup's salespeople and few selected salespeople from the operative units. Together, they win new customers and make the product "sellable" for the sales machine. Typically, this intensive collaboration requires physical co-location.

In most companies, this approach will not be sufficient because it does not change the management system that Core's salespeople are operating in. **In most companies, the scaleup cannot align with Core's sales force unless the system is adjusted.** Adjusting the system is not a methodology issue – it requires dual leadership and adjusting the culture/collaboration (see chapter 5).

There are two levers to adjusting the system: sponsorship from top sales managers and the salespeople's goals and KPIs. The head of sales and the scaleup's executive sponsor should define sales goals that ensure selling the established products and additionally the innovation – for instance, by over-incentivizing selling the new product.

These goals need to be relevant and tangible. Setting the goals in terms of revenues is rarely tangible since there are too many unknowns (e.g., the size of the initial sales and the duration until a follow-on sales). Tangible goals are expressed in customers, e.g., "win 25 customers from a pre-defined market segment."

The scaleup needs dedicated sales resources that run exclusively with the Core's sales units to make this approach work. Touching base only now and then will not lead to success.

International roll-outs

Any scaleup that I worked with had an internationalization strategy, either because the national beachhead market was too small or because target customers are dispersed worldwide. Selecting which international markets to enter, in which sequence, and in which entry mode is a strategic issue. It should never be an opportunistic decision.

Going international adds a layer of complexity to the scaleups' organization. The scaleup needs to:

– establish effective multi-regional sales approaches,

– ensure that proven recipes for success are shared throughout a global salesforce,

– and maintain the repeatability and scalability of the go-to-market and commercial apparatus.

Only a few scaleups succeed in a truly international collaboration with Core's global sales force. I see three barriers quite often. Firstly, **the illusion of local uniqueness.** Typically, Core's regional managers consider their area unique and different from other regions. There are always regional specifics – external ones such as local customer needs and internal ones such as regional assets and capabilities. But this "we are different" view often prevents regional leaders from seeing how importing the innovation may future-proof their regional businesses.

Secondly, non-aligned incentives. Often, there are resourcing and cultural issues. Core's regional leaders typically manage their businesses with tight cost control. They do not have the resources to sell in the innovation and meet their financial performance targets simultaneously. And thirdly, cultural issues. Frequently, there is a "not invented here" mindset and the desire to demonstrate the region's desire to show their ability to operate independently.

Fortunately, none of these barriers are insurmountable. The Lean Scaleup provides a framework for overcoming them by offering a system solution and an innovation infrastructure (see chapter 6) to address global scaling challenges.

Scaling the commercial apparatus

During Scaling-Up, a scalable sales process needs to be developed to power rapid growth, drive down customer acquisition costs, onboard new staff, and learn at pace.

There also needs to be a scalable commercial apparatus that powers and enables this sales process.

In my work with scaleups, I regularly see four questions:

– Which parts of the commercial apparatus (processes, organization, skills, systems/tools, etc.) are already scalable?

– For the parts that are not yet scalable: what would be a scalable setup?

– How could the scaleup build an outbound-sales "machine?"

– How should the scaleup close the gaps (e.g., skill development, new systems/tools, automatization of business processes, etc.)?

Working through these issues requires a model of the commercial apparatus. As an example, for a scaleup client who develops an Internet-Of-Things SAAS solution for a specific industry, the commercial apparatus includes:

– New customer process (from creating awareness to solution delivery/ onboarding)

– Customer development process (key accounts and other accounts)

– Enablers, such as management of contracts and service level agreements, product/service/configuration management, partner management, management of teams and talents, and (customer-facing) innovation management

– Strategy, planning, and controlling comprising issues such as strategy and go-to-market, planning and budgeting, controlling revenue/ cost drivers, and reporting on processes and defined issues

I typically apply a "back from the future" approach and start the design process with a 3-year projection of the business: how many customers and contacts will be there, what is the nature of these customers and contracts, what is the value that the scaleup needs to deliver, what will sales processes look like, etc.

With these hypotheses, which then become part of the scaleup's go-to-market strategy, it is possible to model a scalable commercial apparatus and identify quick wins, the 100-day plan, and longer-running initiatives.

In the context of the "new customer process," scaleups are usually very keen to upgrade their outbound sales. They want to have a "machine" that attracts potential customers and converts them into customers. In my experience, four areas are paramount: target audience and message, process and KPIs, tools, and people.

Message/market-fit (see chapter 7) is not only relevant at the beginning of the innovation journey – **aligning target audience and message** should be a constant concern for the scaleup. Guiding questions regarding **process and KPIs** are, for instance, who is responsible for which stage of the sales funnel and how much technical staff is involved in sales.

Discussions around **tools** should focus on questions like where contacts come from today, how are emails, calls, follow-ups, and sales tracked, which KPIs help to navigate, and which people are involved in a complete sales cycle. When discussing the **people** side of the outbound sales machine, issues like the level of IT affinity, the amount of learning and sharing in the sales team, and end-to-end responsibilities in the sales process should be in the foreground.

Industrializing the product

A scaleup's product-related work is fundamentally different from the product-related work before Scaling-Up. Pre-Scaling, the corporate startup/venture validated that customers saw a product idea (in the business foundation stage) and an MVP (in the business strategy stage) as a clear indication for a yet-to-be-developed superior solution for a high-priority problem.

In the business design stage, customers validated a feature-poor Minimum Marketable Product in their environment.

 In Scaling-Up, there are four categories of product work. Each of these creates value differently:

- Feature work: extending the product's functionality

- Growth work: accelerating product adoption and usage

- Product/market-fit expansion work: expanding the product into an adjacent market, adjacent product, or both.

- Scaling work: developing a scalable, high-performing, solid and secure platform that allows taking on new levels of feature, growth, and product/market-fit expansion work

Clarity prevents problems

I have met scaleups that were not clear about the different product work types. They had no clear view of what is most relevant to the scaleup at any given moment or how they should prioritize work. These scaleups tend to have suboptimal processes, wrong measures of success, and a weak alignment. Any one of these could cause severe problems. If the three of them come together, it might put the entire scaleup ambition is at risk.

It is hard to be effective when clarity is missing. **Sub-optimal engineering management processes** occur when the scaleup manages developments in each of the four kinds of product work the same way. Since every new piece of product work drives technical volume, variance, and complexity, the scaleup may soon find that the engineering pipeline is clogged – leading to a slowdown in product shipment and a growth-limiting impediment for the scaleup.

Each type of product work needs to be measured and managed differently. If the scaleup is not clear on this issue, it will probably apply the **wrong success measures.** For instance, if the Net Promoter Score – the percentage of customers who recommend the product – is the dominant metric, the teams will inevitably focus on "visible results" (e.g., product features) and not on "invisible results" such as scaling work.

A scaleup needs to recognize the value of all different product work types and find the right metrics for all the critical work, not just the outwardly attractive work. Quite understandably, it is exciting to talk about new features because they shine a limelight on the people and teams that do this work. But feature work is only of the four types of product work.

Ultimately, the wrong measures and processes lead to creating the **wrong alignment** – one that focuses on either the wrong type of product work or a sub-optimal portfolio of product work. I have seen scaleups that work on:

– growth when they should be working on feature work. In this case, the scaleup optimizes product usage when it should be improving the product to make it appealing for new customers.

– features when they should be working on growth. In this case, the scaleup overexpands the product's surface area when it should make the product more appealing to existing customers.

– growth or features when they should be working on expanding product/market-fit. Without the latter, the scaleup will not be able to execute on a "bowling alley" growth plan (see above).

– growth or features or expanding product/market-fit when they should be working on technical scaling. By delaying technical scaling, the scaleup will notice that it is becoming increasingly hard to launch new things rapidly.

Feature work

Aside from technical scaling, feature work is the type of work that most people associate with Scaling-Up. In their view, the Minimum Marketable Product is a feature-poor product, and during Scaling-Up, the product will get more and more features to get closer to the product vision. There are many points in this view.

But there are also two critical points that not every scaleup is aware of. Technical work is not primarily about shipping features – there are three other types of product work. And every new feature creates follow-on costs, **"feature shadow costs."** I have seen three prominent types of shadow costs.

Firstly, every new feature creates **maintenance costs**. There is no such thing as zero maintenance. Features must be constantly maintained, updated, and supported no matter how many customers use them. Secondly, new features create **user costs**. Additional functionality increases complexity. Increasing complexity creates friction and impacts users – it can negatively impact feature discovery, new user onboarding, and more.

Thirdly, new features create **killing costs**. The scaleup may think, "we can always kill the feature if it is not popular." But in reality, this is far easier said than done. In my experience, the customers who use features on the periphery of a product are often the power users. They have sophisticated needs and the mindset to adopt new features. Consequently, killing under-used features often impacts power users disproportionately. Because they do not want to make power users unhappy, many scaleups do not kill as many features as they should.

The feature shadow costs are often heavily underestimated. I have seen many product roadmaps show a feature-after-feature-string – but no time for follow-on work and mitigating feature shadows. But when the team ignores feature shadow costs, it may run into problems:

- Lack of focus. The team may be wobbling between initiatives as it discovers that (unplanned) follow-on work is needed, which pulls resources from the roadmap, mandating a constant switching of context for the engineers.

- Complex engineering. With every new feature, product complexity increases, and hence engineering complexity increases.

- Over-engineering. Over-complexity makes it harder for new customers to understand, evaluate and adopt the product. It may even open a market window for more streamlined products.

In my view, there are two keys to winning in feature work. The first one is to keep an eye on feature shadow costs. The other is to ensure that every new feature is part of **a cohesive story**. For example, when Apple launched Touch ID, it seemed strange to many people. But Apple followed up with Apple Wallet and Near-Field Communication, enabling Apple Pay – which is the real story. When I discuss feature work and the scaleup team cannot tell this cohesive story, I usually challenge it by asking, "so why should we be building the feature in the first place?"

Such a cohesive story is fundamental when new use cases require a sizeable behavioral change from customers. The team cannot expect customers to make massive behavior changes instantly – humans do not work that way. Rather than plopping many features into their lap, the team should sequence new features carefully and take their customers on a journey.

I sometimes challenge scaleup teams by discussing "products that were ahead of their time." The question that I put on the table is, "what should the product team have done to lead people through the necessary behavioral changes so that they get value from the product?"

Growth work

Growth work is about increasing customer adoption and improving customer onboarding and customer retention. It creates value by capturing more of the existing customer base. Often, it is much easier to create value (for instance, by leading existing customers into larger and longer-running contracts) than by adding new features and winning new customers.

The critical metrics for growth work are product usage, customer retention, and monetization of the existing product. These work together as a cohesive system for every product, from business-to-consumer social apps and software-as-a-service innovations to enterprise software. Growth work is essential in developing the "full product" that mainstream customers expect (see above).

Growth work is not primarily about more features. **Many scaleups believe that they need to add new features to grow.** A new feature could be the answer to the growth challenge, but often this is not the case. Most product teams know how to develop features, but few understand growth work.

Growth work should not be confused with ruthless optimization and simplification. It could mean, for instance, removing friction in using the product, creating an integration with an adjacent system, improving customer onboarding, or supporting customer roll-out.

When doing growth work, the team needs to understand how the three-part system of product usage, customer retention, and monetization works. With such a model, the team can develop hypotheses about the most significant growth constraints and how to unblock them, test these hypotheses and unlock growth inside the customer base.

Product/market-fit expansion work

At the end of the pre-Scaling phase, a Minimum Marketable Product is available, and the team has validated product/market-fit (see chapter 7). Through feature work and growth work, the scaleup can then capture the initial value potential. But at some point, saturation will slow down growth.

This might not even be a long-term issue – it can come pretty fast. For instance, when the scaleup rapidly wins a large customer base, a snowballing customer base raises the bar of expectations, and the scaleup may not be able to satisfy these increased expectations.

Future growth then depends on **expanding the product/market-fit into other markets** (the "bowling alleys" mentioned above). Product/market fit expansion is not incremental innovation – it is non-incremental and thus an innovation journey in itself.

In chapter 8, I highlighted that product/market-fit is a quality, not an endpoint. Since customer expectations change constantly, the quality of the product/market-fit may go down during Scaling-Up. Consequently, **the scaleup is in a permanent race to achieve a high-quality product/market-fit, defend it, and expand it** – within the existing customer base or with an extended one.

The good news is that the Lean Scaleup methodology (see chapter 7) fully applies to this situation. The team needs to shift the focus from how to solve current customer problems to anticipating how these problems will evolve (for the existing market), or how to transfer existing product/market-fit to new markets. Expanding product/market-fit requires the team to think broader. There are two ways to do this:

- Same product, adjacent market – enabling the product's value proposition for a new market (for example, Slack launching Slack Enterprise)

– Same market, adjacent product – penetrating an existing market with an add-on product (for example, online payment processor Stripe launching Stripe Atlas)

There is one caveat, though. Often, the market sees a fast-growing scaleup as "the new kid on the block," which stands for one great and new product – but not for an extended ambition. Broadening the target audience may create more noise than signal – making it hard not to become distracted.

Scaling work

The art of technical scaling is to find the right timing. If the scaleup is too late in scaling work, an underperforming tech stack becomes an impediment. When limited technical resources are spent better on the other three types of product work instead of scaling, it is too early.

Technical scaling enables the feature, growth, and product/market-fit expansion teams to take on a new threshold. So the technical scalers need to understand what that threshold is to delineate how critical technical performance dimensions – like the number of concurrent users, response times, and bandwidth – will develop. With this information, they are in an excellent position to get the timing of the scaling work right.

Typically, I use four questions to help teams understand the timing challenges of scaling work:

– How much of the team's work on is unplanned firefighting?

– Which opportunities are not pursued because they are too hard to implement?

– Which scaleup priorities didn't get done on time because the team had to clear past "engineering debt?"

– Where does the team need more leverage on its time?

Customer experience is paramount

At the beginning of the Scaling-Up phase, the scaleup should be more obsessed with customer experience than scale. **I advise the CTOs of my scaleup clients to spend time on customer support.** Then, they get first-hand information about what customers like or dislike and what is missing. This helps them to better prioritize the many activities in the four types of product work.

No matter what kind of product the scaleup offers, it is not valuable if the customer experience is painful. I have learned that customers would rather have excellent support and an above-average product than a great product and modest support.

It also helps to ship a fantastic product and a meaningful experience simultaneously. Not every version of the scaleup's product might be of the highest quality right off the bat. As long as the scaleup is crystal-clear on the value and the customer experience it aims to provide, this is something that it can power through.

Chapter

11
SCALING-UP:
PEOPLE AND CULTURE

Six essential insights in this chapter.

You will find these again within the text.

A scaleup needs a growth culture. Such a culture is performance- and learning-oriented, and it also fosters the personal and professional growth of staff.

Top talent such as leading scientists, rockstar business developers, and super-bright Millennials search for an inspiring, creative environment to deliver the best work of their lives.

Seizing the sweet spot of organizational design requires alignment and autonomy at the same time. Autonomy, in turn, requires individual and team accountability.

Aligning autonomous teams with business objectives can be achieved via OKRs (Objectives and Key Results).

The scaleup needs to find suitable candidates, hire the right ones via an excellent recruiting process, and onboard the new hires properly. Many scaleups compromise on at least one of these three.

Falling short on hiring excellence can have severe consequences on the culture.

Controlling excellence starts with selecting what to measure. The focus should be on a few quantifiable factors linked to business success drivers, i.e., leading indicators to future performance.

Two critical metrics that relate to all kinds of scaleups are Customer Lifetime Value and Customer Acquisition Costs.

Scaleups need lean governance with only a few people on the governance board.

Firstly, because of speed. Secondly, there is often a capability problem. Members of corporate committees have a depth of expertise regarding the business model and its functions – but not in new business models or new technologies.

Only a few corporate managers have the personal profile required to build and sustain a hypergrowth organization.

It rarely works because they often prefer to continue pushing on the skills that made them a good corporate manager. It is possible, but it is an entirely new game for those who take on the challenge.

CHAPTER 11

Scaling-Up: People and culture

*"If you get the culture right,
most of the other stuff will just take care of itself."*

Tony Hsieh

A scaleup's people and culture can make or break the big ambition. Culture is a broad, deep, and critical topic and cannot be limited to just one chapter. But since culture and collaboration – both inside the corporate startup/venture or the scaleup and between these and Core – is a fundamental capability for solving a company's business-building problem (see chapter 5), there will be an entire book dedicated to this topic in the future.

This chapter is about the methodology in this topic – the "hard factors" such as recruiting, organizational design principles, and the relationship between scaleup and Core. Due to the inherent incompatibility of Core's system and culture with the systems and cultures of innovation vehicles – corporate startups/ventures and scaleups – there will be inevitable conflicts, as described in chapters 2 and 3. Being aware of these aspects and the levers to pull will help corporate stakeholders and scaleups develop a productive and energizing solution.

At the beginning of the Scaling-Up phase, the scaleup has a few initial customers using the Minimum Marketable Product. Here's the math: suppose these initial customers create an annual revenue of USD 500k. When the scaleup is targeting revenues of USD 10m after three years, this translates into a Compounded Annual Growth Rate (CAGR) of more than 170 percent. If the target is USD 30m after five years, the CAGR is more than 150 percent.

A scaleup with these revenue targets requires an organization far bigger than the one at the beginning of the Scaling-Up phase. Hence, **organizational growth management is as important as making the market and industrializing the product** to succeed. The Lean Scaleup methodology supports corporate stakeholders and scaleups in mastering seven issues that are essential for organizational growth management over 3 to 5 years:

- Identifying people with the proper growth mentality

- Creating a growth culture

- Adding structure without killing the startup

- Finding and onboarding the right hires

- Defining the right metrics for measuring progress

- Designing the scaleup / Core relationship

- Selecting the scaleup leader

The growth mentality

Organizational growth management starts with the growth mentality of the individuals. Hence the scaleup needs to find the right people for a highly dynamic environment and make sure that these understand growth. A growth mentality is not a clever tactic or a one-time team event. There is no silver bullet to get to an annual growth rate of 170 percent and sustain this rate over three years.

Growth mentality comes from the right mindset and the right attitude that people bring to their daily work consistently for years. With a growth mentality, teams can move fast. In my work with scaleups, I have learned that growth mentality has four hallmarks.

Typical scaleups focus the whole day on thinking about the product. They want the product to be noticed and loved by the customer. But thinking about the product is not the same thing as thinking about the customer – although it is easy to mix these two. People with a growth mentality spend more time thinking about the customer than about the product.

They have **empathy for customers**. The question that they have front and center is. "what could we do so that we deserve a place in their complex lives?" People with a growth mentality see themselves directly responsible for growth as part of their job, even if their title says "Product," "Engineering," or "Marketing." In this sense, everyone is on the growth team.

Growth mentality is about **constantly moving with a sense of urgency**. From the very beginning, Amazon's Jeff Bezos implemented a mindset that kept Amazon on a cycle of continuous experimentation, innovation, and optimization. As he said, "it is always day 1. Day 2 is stasis, followed by irrelevance, followed by an excruciating and painful decline, followed by death[69]."

Experiments, measurement, and data are the third part of a growth mentality. If a scaleup wants to grow by 150 percent annually over five years, it must be committed to measuring everything since this is the engine for scalability and growth. Data cannot be an afterthought, and data-driven cannot be a buzzword. Consequently, the scaleup has to devote significant engineering resources to measurement – just as Amazon does, which has data scientists and Artificial Intelligence experts in all business processes, including, for example, recruitment.

Data provides insights into the scaleup's heartbeat; it represents the customer's voice (see above). The key statistics of the scaleup should be on all people's minds. When I start to work with scaleups, I look for the dashboard with the critical KPIs. When I see this dashboard displayed on a big screen on the wall in full view of everyone, I conclude that they take building the business seriously.

A wise scaleup leader makes the team more aggressive in pushing the boundaries than himself/herself. If a manager is in a growth position and the scaleup leader needs to request more experiments instead of vice versa, the manager is in the wrong job.

The last piece of the growth mentality is to **sustain the pain of failure**. Many things that the scaleup tries to grow and scale even faster will not work out. Most new tactics will not be successful. The individuals and the teams need to be able to move on from the losses mentally.

---

69 https://www.aboutamazon.com/news/company-news/2016-letter-to-shareholders

The growth culture

Culture is one of the most overused, yet often least understood, concepts in business. I like to think **of culture as the employees' shared beliefs of the rules** concerning "us and them" (belonging and being different), emotional safety, and success:

- What do I need to do to be "in" (and not out)?

- What are the behaviors so that I can feel emotionally safe?

- What do I need to do so that others see me as a winner?

A scaleup's culture can make or break any Scaling-Up ambition. To paraphrase Stan Slap[70], it is an independent organism living right inside the company. The scaleup's leadership team cannot bribe, bluff, or bully the culture into sustainably doing or believing anything if the culture is unwilling to "buy it." But a culture is also a rational system that will catapult the scaleup on its journey if the leadership team gives it what it wants first.

So, I doubt that it is good enough when the sole goal is building a company that sells products to a snowballing customer base. In my view, the chances for success are much higher when the scaleup aims at rapid growth combined with creating a legacy – "making a dent in the universe," as Steve Jobs once said – and impacting the lives of the people that help achieve this overarching goal.

In my view, **the crucial word is growth**. Growth is not just the outcome in terms of revenues or the size of the organization. Growth also refers to individual growth. People want to be in a work environment that allows them to grow personally and professionally by collaborating with other great people.

Top talent such as leading scientists, rockstar business developers, and super-bright Millenials are not incentivized by "instrumental psychology." They search for the most inspiring, creative environment to deliver the best work of their lives.

---

70 Stan Slap, "Under the Hood"

When the scaleup does not have such a growth culture, it might fail on both ends. It might not attract and retain top talent – hence it loses steam, loses in the market, and ultimately loses company support. But it may as well also blow itself up in hypergrowth, operating in frantic chaos while confusing customers and the company.

On the surface, successful scaleups share many cultural similarities that one can think of as the manifestation of a growth culture:

–   Ambition to create a company that has a positive impact on the world and does so at scale

–   Extreme determination to reach growth targets

–   Competitive stance towards other providers of the product

–   Risk-taking to introduce new approaches or processes

–   Courage to take bold actions and make improvements happen

–   Cohesion, togetherness, and a "company spirit"

–   Diversity in people's expertise and backgrounds, perspectives, and ways of thinking

–   Resilience in responding to crises and keep the soul of the scaleup alive in challenging times

When I co-created the Lean Scaleup framework with more than 20 industry-leading companies, we asked ourselves, "how could a scaleup build such a growth culture?" We wanted to find the methodology – but not with the intent to create instrumental psychology. Rather, we searched for actionable levers to help scaleup leaders with the right mindset (see above) to create such a culture.

We started by distinguishing a growth culture from other cultures. A growth culture is **not a performance-oriented culture**. The latter, which often prevails in Core, focuses on results. It exacerbates people's fears via a zero-sum game in which people succeed or fail – "losers" get quickly get weeded out from "winners." A growth culture is also **not a learning culture**. Learning cultures focus more on building and sharing knowledge and expertise sharing than creating tangible, measurable results.

A growth culture integrates aspects of these two types of culture. Like the performance culture, it is result-oriented – otherwise, the scaleup could not meet the challenging growth goals. Like the learning culture, a growth culture puts building and sharing knowledge on top of the list – but these are a means to an end, i.e., meeting the growth goals.

But a growth culture goes beyond these. It focuses on deeper issues connected to how people feel and how they behave because this will liberate the team's energy. In a growth culture, how people feel and make other people feel becomes as important as how much they know or their results. In the view of the Lean Scaleup co-creators, such a growth culture rests on six pillars.

In a growth culture, people build their capacity to see through blind spots. They **acknowledge failures, insecurities, and shortcomings** rather than unconsciously acting them out. A growth culture provides a psychologically safe environment in which people spend less energy demonstrating or defending their individual value – and consequently, they have more power available to create external value.

A growth culture requires a **delicate balance between challenging and nurturing**. Too much challenge over a 3-to-5-year period without sufficient reassurance may overwhelm the individuals and break the organization. Too little challenge, or too much time in the comfort zone of slow but steady growth, will put the growth goals at risk and eventually create a "steady development" culture, which might be too small for the company's ambition.

To accelerate growth, **continuous learning with real-time feedback** is essential. Real-time feedback could come from experts, peers, partners, competitors, or, most importantly, customers. Scaleups with a growth culture rely heavily on objective data that supports quantified feedback.

Psychologists assert that we all construct "mental models" to make sense of our experiences and inform our decisions. In a growth culture, people strive to have **concise mental models** – the best way of explaining things and the best beliefs, insights, and assumptions upon which the team builds hypotheses for what works in Scaling-Up. Concise mental models must be short and straightforward. If they are not, they will not help people learn rapidly. But when the scaleup's mental models are concise, short, simple, and validated, they can become both a factor for success and a vital part of the scaleup's corporate identity and culture.

All of us have **different learning styles**. I am an auditive person, and I learn from podcasts and audiobooks. Other people are visual or kinesthetic and prefer different learning styles. Rapid learning in a growth culture, therefore, needs to build on a variety of approaches. Storytelling (see chapter 8) is effective because it creates the context for mental models.

Research suggests that the optimal size for a business team with a defined end-to-end responsibility is about five to seven persons and should not go beyond eight or nine – Amazon's famous "two pizza rule." These numbers allow for **effective teamwork**. They ensure a diversity of perspectives and skills but are small enough to prevent the group from subdividing and reduce communication costs and miscommunication risks. Because rapid growth is highly collaborative and interdisciplinary, no individual will have all the necessary knowledge, relevant mental models, or insights. The goal is to assemble teams whose members have a shared vision but complementary skills and varied viewpoints.

A culture that builds on these six pillars empowers people. For example, one of my scaleup clients did an internal hackathon to upgrade a customer-relevant process. The CEO called staff to pitch ideas and said the management team would investigate further the top ten ideas. Three of these ten ideas came from the receptionist.

Adding structure without killing the startup

When it comes to organizational structure, the scaleup's challenge is to avoid becoming what it wants to disrupt: an established company with formal processes and a risk-averse mentality. I usually start discussions about the structure for the next level of the scaleup's growth with a simple visual (see next page).

Two crucial dimensions for designing a scaleup's organization are **autonomy and speed (respectively, available time).** If there is too much autonomy, the teams create works of art (e.g., one brilliant feature after the other) or chaos, depending on the available time. With too little autonomy, teams run experiments forever or work like a sausage machine (highly efficient but unable to adapt to a highly dynamic environment) depending on the available time.

 None of these four extremes is optimal. I think the optimum is the sweet spot in the middle. For seizing it, **alignment and accountability are essential**. At first, autonomy and alignment may seem to be contradictory and two extremes on a scale. But an agile scaleup organization needs both.

Successful scaleups and fast-growing "new" companies like Spotify or Amazon spend a lot of time and effort on getting the autonomy/alignment balance right. They operate – except for highly standardized tasks such as picking articles in an Amazon logistics center – on small autonomous teams. Amazon calls these two pizza teams (see above). **The more aligned a scaleup's organization is, the more autonomy it can grant to its teams.**

Figure 11-1: The sweet spot in organizational design

Achieving autonomy and alignment at the same time requires empowering and coaching teams. A frequently chosen way is to ensure that teams internalize the business vision and objectives and then align their deliverables with the business objectives. Many scaleups had an excellent experience with this approach, the so-called OKR method (Objectives and Key Results).

Autonomy does not come without accountability. Unlike responsibility, accountability cannot be shared. In the growth culture (see above), people are empowered to make decisions. But they are also accountable for the outcome of those decisions – in a non-blaming way. When a decision's results are questionable, there should be a review process that explores why people got there and what they learned from it. So in a way, **autonomy is learned and earned**.

In my view, this sweet spot is the fertile ground from which **individual and team commitment** grow. Commitment can be measured by "share of shower[71]" – what percentage of time would staff spend in an environment that is a hotbed of creativity on the scaleup's business challenges? If a young and vibrant scaleup can manifest and sustain such a high share of shower in an autonomy/alignment culture, it can really "change the order of things" (see chapter 3) and "make a dent in the universe," as Steve Jobs said.

As the scaleup grows, it becomes increasingly difficult to add new people because the learning curve starts to get steep. **Specialization and adding management layers are not the panacea in autonomy/alignment organizations.** Specialization seems to be the natural decision when the company size grows, but it comes with a price: more hand-offs across groups, potentially conflicting agendas, and specialized knowledge rather than knowledge-sharing. So this, in turn, would suggest installing management structures that coordinate the specialists.

It might be more effective to embed the managers into the autonomy/alignment teams. There is an old debate in the agile expert community if small teams ("squads") should have managers or not and if ownership of the objectives should sit within or outside the teams. Agile experts suggest that

---

71 https://www.hiltonbarbour.com/hiltonbarbourblog/shareofshower

squads with a team-inside manager tend to be more resilient to fast change than teams with a team-outside manager.

When the number of autonomous/aligned teams becomes too large and additional structures are needed, I advise my scaleup clients to think of structures as the **communication architecture.** Any structure optimizes communication among some parts of the organization at other parts' expense. For example, if product management is in the engineering organization, communication between product management and engineering will be optimized, but at the expense of communication between product management and marketing.

A "communication architecture" view also relates to how the company communicates with the outside world. For example, the scaleup may want to organize its sales force by product groups to maximize communication with the technical product groups and maximize the sales force's product competency. But if it does that, it will be at the expense of simplicity for customers who buy multiple products and now have to deal with various salespeople.

Finding and onboarding the right hires

In an established company, teams are a given. A new manager might be happy or struggle with the team, but there are people available to deliver what is required. A fundamental challenge for any scaleup is attracting top talent to join its mission. This talent might join the scaleup for a limited time or permanently.

Because time is of the essence, I advise my scaleup clients to have an on-demand pool of **interim top talent** to cover short-term challenges and recruitment gaps. Some of my corporate clients also have a self-managed pool of "entrepreneurs-in-residence." These are business builders who have experienced Scaling-Up challenges and know how to address them. Other corporate clients engage with specialized service providers to get access to seasoned experts on demand.

When it comes to hiring, there are three challenges. The scaleup needs to find suitable candidates, hire the right ones via an excellent recruiting process, and onboard the new hires properly. Many scaleups compromise on at least one of these three.

Falling short on hiring excellence can have severe consequences. When the company size grows from 20 to 120 in a year's space, seemingly overnight new employees can vastly outnumber the original team. This dynamic can permanently redefine the corporate culture because "**new people are hiring new people to hire new people.**"

The right people can be 400 percent more productive in "normal" jobs than average employees and 800 percent in demanding jobs[72]. As Steve Jobs said, "a small team of A+ players can run circles around a giant team of B and C players."

One example of such an A+ player is Amazon's Charlie Ward. He envisioned the idea of Amazon Prime while working as an engineer. More than 150 million customers in 17 countries are now customers of the Amazon Prime subscription service, a USD 19bn business for Amazon. Charlie Ward is still with Amazon, currently a VP of Technology.

Amazon's **recruiting process** finds people like Charlie Ward and wins them for the company. It is a radical alternative to the home-grown approaches that many scaleups use. Home-grown recruiting typically falls short in two ways:

- Interviewers' skills – they are at a crucial point in the recruiting process. Still, they typically lack a rigorous model for their role in recruiting and the training to assess the candidate's likely job performance.

- Process design - internal discussions about candidates often lack clarity, opening the door for confirmation bias and other traps that feel right but produce poor decisions.

---

72 https://www.mckinsey.com/business-functions/organization/our-insights/attracting-and-retaining-the-right-talent

Time pressure explains suboptimal recruiting processes, up to a point. According to Sequoia Capital[73], the average startup in Silicon Valley spends 990 hours hiring 12 software engineers. In other words, the average recruiting time per hire is two workweeks – time taken from a team that is already understaffed and struggles to meet the deadlines. But if a scaleup wants to create a growth culture to meet its ambitions, **it must find the time to design and implement an excellent recruiting process.** My clients who apply the Lean Scaleup at level 3 (see chapter 6) use the company builder to ensure recruiting excellence.

Successful scaleups also onboard new hires effectively. A robust onboarding process ensures that every new hire understands how the scaleup works at a certain level of detail – because that is the only way that new hires can make an impact. **A robust onboarding process is a foundational piece for enabling growth.**

Since working at a scaleup is stressful, the average annual employee churn rate is 25 percent[74] - so if the goal is to increase staff size from 100 to 200 in two years and the scaleup has an average churn rate, it needs to recruit 150 people and not 100. With proper onboarding, retention increases by 82 percent and productivity by over 70 percent[75]. This insight is crucial because it is difficult to achieve (much less survive) hypergrowth if the scaleup constantly replaces team members.

Measuring progress – Scaleup metrics

Performance measurement and target-setting are vital to the growth process. A scaleup is not just a small company that might get by without much formal progress control or target-setting. Hypergrowth requires the scaleup to build an excellent control process.

Knowing business performance in terms of revenues, free cash flow, and the bottom line is valuable information. But an excellent control process

---

73 "Recruit Engineers in Less Time," Sequoia, https://www.sequoiacap.com/article/recruit-engineers-in-less-time/.
74 https://www.founderscircle.com/high-startup-turnover-rate/
75 https://b2b-assets.glassdoor.com/the-true-cost-of-a-bad-hire.pdf

needs to well beyond these dimensions. It needs to put the scaleup leader in a position where they can manage the high-dynamics of the business proactively.

Controlling excellence starts with selecting what to measure. The focus should be on a few **quantifiable metrics linked to leading indicators of future business performance.**

These factors do not include so-called vanity metrics – things the scaleup can measure and create some excitement (like the top position on Google's search rankings) but do not predict future business.

Core's sophisticated controlling dimensions to measure productivity and success in an established business model do not help. The scaleup's context is entirely different, and measurements such as Discounted Cash Flow, Internal Rate of Return, or Return On Capital Employed in Core's full-blown controlling system rarely help a scaleup.

One crucial measurement focuses on how the scaleup is doing with its most valuable customers, i.e., the customers with the highest **Customer Lifetime Value** (CLV). If the average CLV is not higher than the projected **Customer Acquisition Cost (CAC)**, the scaleup will flame out. The best scaleups that I have worked with review leading and lagging indicators for CLV at segment level every day, using sophisticated analytical tools that show customer churn signs.

Some excellent scaleups also see Core as one of the most valuable customers. Their KPI system contains measures that relate to the essential pain points of the company's customers. With this setup, the scaleup can receive sustained support from the operative units because it helps them reach their goals.

Scaleup / Core relationship

Chapter 5 showed that "dual leadership" and "culture/collaboration" are essential for solving the corporate business-building problem. In my experience, designing the interface between Core and scaleup is most straight-forward when both sides think of this as **building a shared infrastructure that respects their operating models** (see chapter 2).

This infrastructure contains four elements:

– Startup-ish autonomy with corporate understanding

– Defined collaboration model

– Defined executive support

– Adequate risk management

With the Lean Scaleup framework, the first three issues are relatively straightforward and have already been covered more or less in this book. However, the last dimension typically leads to intensive discussions, especially concerning governance and funding.

Lean governance

In Core, committees usually govern cross-silo initiatives. Aside from decision-making, these committees also help to achieve consensus and maintain the political balance. For corporate initiatives that span across many silos, governance committees can be sizable. Typically, these committees are slow-moving. They meet monthly or quarterly and require decision papers two weeks in advance.

 Such an approach will not work for scaleups. On the one hand, because of speed. Scaleups are fast-moving units, perma-nently racing against the clock to reach the next business-building milestone before the competition and before corporate funding and support flame out.

On the other side, there is a capability problem. Members of corporate committees have deep expertise regarding the business model and the relevant functions – but not necessarily in new business models or new technologies.

Consequently, Core and scaleup need to think carefully about which corporate stakeholder should be on the governance board. A good starting point is to look at the closeness to the existing business and the scaleup's anticipated future home after Scaling-Up.

If the scaleup targets existing customers and should be re-integrated after Scaling-Up into one of Core's operating business units, the respective stakeholder must be on the governance board. If the scaleup targets new customers and should become a separate legal entity after Scaling-Up, it should instead be the Chief Strategy Officer who goes on the governance board.

Metered funding

Chapter 5 showed that a VC-type approach to scaleup funding – earmarked funding combined with the release of funding as the scaleup meets pre-defined milestones – is the best way. It provides safety and stability for the scaleup, top talent, and Core's risk management.

Typically, these milestones are multi-dimensional and come from the Scaling-Up workstreams above. They relate to:

- Making the market (revenues, acquired lighthouse customers, progress in the bowling alley, traction metrics, etc.)

- Industrializing the product (product development concerning versions/features, scaling work, etc.)

- Growing the organization (e.g., size of the company, number of open positions, etc.)

With such a setup, monthly meetings between the scaleup and the governance board could be more of an "operational sponsor meeting" than a formal steering committee meeting. Some scaleups that I have worked with started monthly meetings with a list of the five things they needed, rather than a progress update, and quarterly meetings with top executives of the parent company turned into discussion sessions on the long-term vision.

Manage corporate expectations about 'the plan'

In the core organization, managers win when they develop effective plans to reach business goals and execute flawlessly. Quite rightly, this approach is the predominant model to exploit a proven business model.

Many corporate stakeholders think that this model is also the right one to create a new business from innovation. However, finding a new, sustainable business model and building a new business is fundamentally different from exploiting an existing business model (see chapter 2). One cannot put into a spreadsheet how people are going to behave around a new product. **There is no point in trying to make the world match the spreadsheet.**

I have witnessed many tough discussions between corporate stakeholders and scaleups about "the team falling short on the plan." The problem with "the plan" often begins in the pre-Scaling phase. Corporate stakeholders often push corporate startups/ventures to think big. They ask them to put together a revenue plan that delivers an ambitious revenue goal – a goal so big that it is relevant to the Board of Directors and the shareholders. And they request the team to develop a plan for how to reach this ambitious goal.

This "back from the future" approach might work in existing markets where customers understand what the product does and compare it with current alternatives. But this approach does not work in markets that do not yet exist.

Additionally, many companies overlook that the overall market does not adopt a superior solution linearly. Mainstream customers, which represent the most significant part of the market value (and the large numbers under the "hockey stick curve" in the revenue plan), adopt new technology fundamentally different than pioneers and early adopters (see chapter 9).

Customer growth in Scaling-Up is hardly linear because of "the chasm" between pioneers/early adopters and mainstream customers. In reality, growth is even slower than the "Crossing the Chasm" framework suggests. It assumes that at 50 percent of the Scaling-Up journey, the scaleup has won 50 percent of its Serviceable Available Market (SAM). But statistics tell that the average scaleup has won only 10 percent of its SAM[76] at half-time of its Scaling-Up journey. Consequently, "the plan" is often a fantasy from day one.

---

76 https://www.thetriplechasm.com/post/customergrowth

Scaleup leadership

Regularly, I discuss the leadership team profiles of scaleups – apart from the obvious, functional capabilities – with my corporate clients. Quite often, they suggest putting experienced corporate managers at the top of the helm.

Outstanding scaleup leaders have a great sense of ownership – they own everything in their scaleup. They own the successes and the defeats – and blame no one else. This might sound very simplistic, but there lies the fascination of business-building in the corporate context. "Leading a scaleup is easy as riding a bicycle," one scaleup leader said to me. "But you have to know that the bicycle burns and everything else burns as well."

At heart, leading a scaleup is about entrepreneurship in uncharted waters. The scaleup leader needs to determine where to go, how to get there, who should be on the team and lead the team to get there. This team creates products that have never been built before and races against time to win in the market and to maintain corporate support.

To grow, a scaleup leader must take risks and constantly put themselves in new, challenging, and increasingly ambiguous settings. Experience will help navigate these new roads only so far. New challenges that come with every new growth step require new approaches and skills. Additionally, these challenges do not come linearly: when a scaleup grows from 10 to 85 people in one year, the dynamic changes, and it is a new game.

Due to the high pace and dynamics, the scaleup leader will inevitably find that proven methods in Core – such as titles and hierarchies – do not work for a scaleup. "Leaders" will emerge in the organization that do not have the most prominent title but a significant impact. That impact can be a connector, a champion in their function, or a collaborator.

The scaleup leader must be humble, highly self-aware, have a thirst for self-improvement, and be able to hold things loosely so that they can quickly recalibrate. To scale themself, the leader needs to recruit managers who can work and thrive in a highly dynamic environment. Some of these hires will come from outside, with a different mindset. The scaleup leader needs to learn to trust these people, even when they do not have the full context.

Simultaneously, the scaleup leader must work constructively with corporate stakeholders to ensure ongoing support, funding, and resources. That implies investing time in understanding and addressing corporate concerns while also having sufficient diplomatic skills to challenge corporate orthodoxies.

For these reasons, I am skeptical that most corporate managers would be effective scaleup leaders. It rarely works because they often prefer to continue pushing on the skills that made them a good corporate manager.

But it is possible. I have met great corporate managers who became outstanding scaleup leaders. But it is an entirely new game for those who take on the challenge.

Chapter

12
OUTLOOK

CHAPTER 12

Outlook

"If one does not know to what port he is steering,
no wind is favorable to him."

Lucius Annaeus Seneca

Management attention on getting business-building from innovation right has sharply increased in the last four years. Some companies made bold moves, such as bp and Robert Bosch, who set up "Scaling-Up factories" outside their Core's walls. Other companies have installed Scaling-Up functions and "New Business" business units inside the organization that scale validated corporate startups/ventures.

These companies are pioneers in business-building excellence. Turning Scaling-Up from art into practice has just begun. Building the company's business-building capability – or, as some of my clients say, "scaling Scaling-Up" will enter the mainstream in the following years. An increasing number of companies will build the three capabilities needed to succeed – methodology, dual leadership, and culture/collaboration (see chapter 5) – and develop their specific "innovation infrastructure beyond the lab" (see chapter 6).

When time permits, my corporate clients and I discuss what will come next on the corporate agenda regarding building a business from innovation. I see three topics that have the potential to become an "Emerging Practice," i.e., provide companies with a competitive advantage.

Strategic fruit flies

The accelerating pace of change and connectedness in the economy and society has created a more complex set of Corporate Strategies' challenges. In many companies, corporate strategy is changing. The **traditional scope of strategy has expanded** – today, it comprises the classic annual forecasting, planning, and budgeting, in addition to M&A, investor communications, business transformation, and corporate and social responsibility.

Companies also **change the way by which they create strategy**:

– The classic two step-approach – strategy development first, then strategy execution – is augmented with strategic experimentation to validate fundamental assumptions about strategic options

– Corporate strategy is opening to participation by all levels of the organization and ecosystem partners

– Short strategy sprints augment annual cycles

– Big Data and Artificial Intelligence tools enhance strategic insight and decision-making

The Chief Strategy Officer now has a different job to do, sometimes described as managing the business's vitality. They should take the lead in embedding scaleup capabilities into business units as a critical part of the new added value from strategy.

Some of my clients are working towards aligning innovation and their strategic renewal by having a fresh look at strategic options from leveraging corporate assets (see chapter 2). This ambition requires a unit that simultaneously addresses external customers and internal capabilities. Existing innovation centers or digital labs do not fulfill this role *per se* – but they can be developed into such a unit.

This development builds on **explorative strategic experiments**. Via these experiments, options with a business foundation (see chapter 7) are explored and validated. The big difference with conventional strategic work is that the whole approach is not only top-down and not only based on statistics (which do not tell the entire story anyhow, see chapter 9).

The bottom-up augmentation of strategy work with real-life experiments is new for many senior managers. When one client visited the project room and saw the wall with all the post-its representing dozens of these small experiments and the buzz in the room about all those experiments, he called it the "fruit fly approach." I think this is a good description of what is going on.

In genetics research, fruit flies (*drosophila melanogaster*) are a fantastic model. They are cheap to breed, their reproduction cycle is fast, their genetic code is simple, and they share 8,000 out of their 14,000 genes with humans. In the "fruit fly approach," quick and cheap experiments uncover and validate value pools.

These "fruit fly" experiments provide a validated business foundation within three months and reduce the options that should go into the pre-Scaling's business strategy and later stages (see chapter 7). Even if senior managers kill a fruit fly, there is still value. The learning and insight are relevant for innovation and Core's marketing and business development departments.

Additionally, the fruit fly approach can energize corporate intrapreneurship programs. Intrapreneurs learn to work faster with precisely delimited targets. They might even jump from one experiment to another, carrying on the best practices and insights from previous ones.

Integration of Operations and Innovation

Software development has influenced innovation in at least two crucial aspects. Agile work styles have become the *de facto* work style in pre-Scaling (and to a large extent, also in Scaling-Up). And the software design paradigm of APIs (application programming interfaces) provides **a thinking model of how to leverage corporate assets for innovation**.

I see an interesting trajectory in software development that may find its way into innovation. In some companies, the boundaries between the "delivery engine" (corporate IT) and the "innovation engine" (Digital labs and scaleups) blur. One common characteristic of these companies is that they require their scaleups to dock the scaleup's product to Core's systems during Scaling-Up – for example, to ensure a company-wide risk and fraud model.

During Scaling-Up, these companies set up mixed teams, staffed by people from corporate IT and the scaleup's technical team. With proper governance and a rigorous system for prioritizing and delivering technology work, the tensions between delivery and innovation can be turned into value. A recent study[77] showed that companies who follow this approach are 50 percent less likely to face issues in integrating new digital efforts with their core IT architecture.

In my view, the blurring of delivery/operations and innovations in transactional IT and Digital IT is an early signal for how companies could organize for business-building in the future: **mixed teams from both sides that collaborate on Scaling-Up issues temporarily and then dissolve.**

In this context, I think it is also relevant that modern software tools allow companies to dive deep into their informal networks. These tools analyze organizational networks to find, for example, connectors and influencers. In one company, the analysis found that 3 percent of company staff drive the perceptions of 90 percent and highlighted the people who should be involved to make the company 25 percent more agile.

A holistic view on the Three Playing Fields

Chapters 2 and 3 showed that companies need an operating model for all three Playing Fields in which they operate. Playing Field 2, "Reshape the Core," is the one in which Scaling-Up takes place. Scaling-Up requires resources from the scaleup and Core's corporate assets to materialize an unfair advantage and accelerate the journey – hence there should only be a limited number of concurrent scaleups (see chapter 5).

---

77 https://www.mckinsey.com/business-functions/mckinsey-digital/our-insights/toward-an-integrated-technology-operating-model

I think companies will adopt a Three Playing Field view in their resource and portfolio management more and more commonly to prevent capacity bottlenecks. The Lean Scaleup can help these companies by providing a language and improving the visibility on every corporate startup/venture, all scaleups, and the corporate assets that these use.

In this sense, the Lean Scaleup is also a building block for a state-of-the-art portfolio management system that spans all of the company's three Playing Fields. It helps the company to win in all three plays, in "Optimizing the Core," "Reshaping the Core," and in "Creating the New."

INDEX

C

Q

R

Printed in Poland
by Amazon Fulfillment
Poland Sp. z o.o., Wrocław
28 March 2022

21697af3-25e9-41bd-a811-b73fb825cfb1R02